PET AUTHORPRENEUR 101

HOW TO BECOME A SUCCESSFUL PET AUTHOR AND GROW YOUR BUSINESS

WENDY VAN DE POLL

SPIRIT PAW PRESS, LLC

Pet Authorpreneur 101:
How to Become a Successful Pet Author and
Grow Your Business

Copyright © 2019 Wendy Van de Poll

All rights reserved. No part of this publication may be reproduced, distributed, or transmitted in any form or by any means, including photocopying, recording, or other electronic or mechanical methods, without the prior written permission of the publisher, except in the case of brief quotations embodied in reviews and certain other non-commercial uses permitted by copyright law.

Published by Spirit Paw Press, LLC

Publisher's Cataloging-in-Publication Data
provided by Five Rainbows Cataloging Services

Names: Van de Poll, Wendy, author.
Title: Pet authorpreneur 101 : how to become a successful pet author and grow your business / Wendy Van de Poll.
Description: Concord, NH : Spirit Paw Press, 2020. | Series: Pet biz, bk. 3. | Also available in ebook format.
Identifiers: ISBN 978-1-7324375-5-5 (paperback)
Subjects: LCSH: Pets. | Self-publishing. | Authorship--Handbooks, manuals, etc. | Authorship--Vocational guidance. | Authorship--Marketing. | BISAC: LANGUAGE ARTS & DISCIPLINES / Writing / Authorship. | PETS / General.
Classification: LCC PN161 .V36 2020 (print) | LCC PN161 (ebook) | DDC 808.02--dc23.

THANK YOU

THANK YOU

A Free Gift

Thank you for purchasing *Pet Authorpreneur 101: How to Become a Successful Pet Author and Grow Your Business*. To show my appreciation, I am offering a free gift to help you as a new or experienced pet author.

A Winning Checklist
~ Become a Successful Pet Author and
Grow Your Business ~

Your Link to receive your Free Gift!

https://wendyvandepoll.com/pet-authorpreneur-free-checklist

*To the animals that enrich my life
with their words.*

CONTENTS

SECTION I
GET READY TO WRITE

1. What do You Want to Write About?	3
2. Create Your Avatar	14
3. Mind Mapping Techniques	26
4. Outlining Your Manuscript	39
5. Character Profiles For Fiction	45

SECTION II
READY. SET. WRITE.

6. Make Time for Writing Every Day	53
7. Motivation, Inspiration, and Procrastination	66
8. Your Rough Draft	80
9. Clean up Your Rough Draft	88

SECTION III
WHAT'S NEXT FOR SUCCESS

10. Find Your Editors	103
11. Design Your Book	110
12. Create a Website and Landing Page	119
13. Build a Launch Team	130
14. Kindle Direct Publishing	140
15. Internet Marketing	146
16. In Person Marketing	156
Pep Talk!	164
Glossary	167
Resources	171
Acknowledgements	178

About the Author	179
Thank You!	181
Also by Wendy Van de Poll	183

SECTION I

GET READY TO WRITE

Are you wondering where to begin? Before starting a book, there are some preparations you need to make.

This section is about how you determine the purpose for your book, create your avatar, and mind map your ideas. It is both for the newbie and seasoned author.

I will:

- Help you get organized to begin and improve your project
- Show you the preliminary steps to take before you even type that first letter

If you are nervous about writing, please take a deep breath. This section is about preparation, the preliminary period before writing a book. It will get you into the right frame of mind to apply yourself and create an amazing manuscript.

Please know you have everything it takes to create a great book—even if you have never written one before, you do not have an English degree, or if your grammar made your English teachers wince in school (mine did).

You do not need to be an expert to write a book for pet lovers and/or professionals. All you need is a deep love of animals, a desire to share your thoughts and stories with other people, plus some great people on your team (Section III).

The second thing is to lower your expectations of yourself. Perfectionism is a sure way to kill your inspiration and develop writer's block. The first draft of your book does not have to be the world's most stunning dissertation.

In fact, it is guaranteed to be a bit messy and rough. The important thing is to believe in yourself and get your ideas down. From there, you will be able to smooth out your manuscript (Glossary) and utilize an excellent team of editors, proofreaders, cover designers, and the like to help your book reach its full potential.

Last but not least, find your inspiration. Your inspiration is your heart's passion and the message you want to share with your readers. This will be your biggest motivator. It will also help you overcome fear and apply yourself to the task of writing. Even on days when you want to give up or you start thinking that writing is not for you, your inspiration will whisper in your ear, "You have to get your idea out into the world!"

1
WHAT DO YOU WANT TO WRITE ABOUT?

People say, 'What advice do you have for people who want to be writers?' I say, they do not really need advice, they know they want to be writers, and they are gonna do it. Those people who know that they really want to do this and are cut out for it, they know it.
— R.L. Stine

What do you want to write? This question may seem absurdly simple, but it is critical to ask yourself before you even begin.

Maybe you already roughly know what you want to write, but now is the time to solidify your desire into a true topic (non-fiction) and/or plot (fiction) for your book. Once you know what you want to write, you can begin to develop and map your ideas into a cohesive whole that takes shape into a great book.

Find Your Purpose

To begin, you will need to determine: Why is the topic you want to write about important? How is it going to help or entertain your reader, and/or solve a problem they may have? Think about the purpose before you even open up your word processor or put pen to paper.

The thing is, a book has to have a purpose. Otherwise, you won't be able to attract readers. Having a clear purpose:

- Guides you through the writing process
- Keeps you on task with your writing
- Motivates and inspires you
- Attracts readers and holds their attention
- Makes marketing a snap

When you begin writing, you can start the process by carefully selecting a topic aligned with your purpose and then outline what you plan to address about the topic.

Before you start your manuscript, be clear with what you want to share with your readers. You can cover many topics related to your purpose in your book, but the topics should all be linked in some way.

Having a book about many unrelated subjects is too scattered; if you have two drastically different topics, consider separating them into two different books. Let me phrase this in another way: Select one topic for your book and then cover all of the related subtopics that you want within its pages.

Are You Ready?

It is time to delve into your soul and locate your purpose for writing. Ask yourself if your book is going to be:

- A passion project, where you share stories or aid a cause
- An educational book to help pet owners
- A collection of true stories, or completely fictional
- Something to go along with your business (nonfiction) or something you want to create because you have a story in your heart (fiction)

There are many different topics to write about regarding animals. You can write fiction stories about adorable talking cats or true stories about your amazing seeing-eye companion. You can write informational guides to help pet owners provide the best care to their beloved friends. Or you can write books centered around causes, such as raising awareness about common training and care practices that harm horses.

There are two main things to consider—are you passionate about this topic, and do you have your purpose? Writing a book is an arduous task, so you should not write about things that you care little about.

If you don't care about your topic, you will probably lose motivation long before you complete Chapter 1. But when you have passion to drive you, you will be willing and able to do what is needed and have fun while writing. You will be able to find the motivation to complete your book, and readers will be able to feel your enthusiasm through your written words.

I am sure, as an animal lover and/or professional, you have many pet topics you are passionate about. If you run a pet business, that is a good clue about the part of the pet industry you care deeply about.

Look at what drives you and what you want to share, then write about that. Ask your clients—if you have a business—if they have a burning issue they cannot solve. You can also do research on Amazon to determine what fiction and nonfiction animal books are bestsellers.

Your book should center around a story. This could be:

- A story you made up for fiction
- A story from your own life or one you heard while working in the pet industry
- A common story about pets that everyone could relate to
- A story about how to care for pets to avoid ill health, injury, abuse, neglect, and other tragedies
- A story that is personal or general

Ask yourself, "What story do I want to tell? Why do I want to tell it?" That story must have some sort of message that changes readers' lives or entertains in some way.

Remember how the best books you have read touched your heart and soul? And you think of them long after you reach the final period and set them down. You might even reread books because you love the message so much.

To write a great book that people love, you must deliver a message they will remember after they finish reading. Even heartwarming pet fiction has a deeper message. Ask yourself:

- What message you want to impart to other people
- How you want your readers to feel and do after setting your book down
- What you want people to learn from your book

Example

Charlotte's Web is an example of how a story delivers a powerful message. If you are like me, then you shed more than a few tears over that book. I am not saying your book must become a tear-jerking, award-winning saga that becomes a staple of children's reading experience. I am saying your book's purpose must somehow affect readers in a way to match your desired intent.

My pet loss grief books (https://amazon.com/author/wendy-vandepoll) support people all over the world when going through the loss of a pet. I get beautiful and heartfelt messages in my inbox on a daily basis telling me how my books have helped my readers.

A book is a powerful thing. You can change lives with it as you educate other people about your thoughts. It is a way to express yourself and leave a lasting imprint on the world.

If you want to write and publish a book you can be proud of and feel good about, find your heart's passion. It is the best way to accomplish this goal.

Dare to be Unique

There is no right or wrong topic when writing about animals! The fact you want to write a book to begin with is commendable. Lots of people want to write a book—but you are actually taking action! You are accomplishing something amazing. This book will be your baby—create it the way you want.

This means you should not focus on what you think people want or what the current trends are—unless you have an interest in writing about those things. It really depends on your goals for self-publishing.

Find your own unique voice and story, then offer the world something they cannot get from any other book. You must share something that matters to you because chances are it will matter to other people.

When I first started my site, centerforpetlossgrief.com, I knew I wanted to help people recover from the heartbreak of losing a beloved family pet. This issue is a major one for animal lovers and professionals, yet it is seldom addressed in the pet industry. I knew I would find readers who were looking for heartfelt, compassionate help while navigating grief. People wanted someone who understood and acknowledged their pain. Instead of looking at precedented businesses, I created something totally original and offered people a service they could not find many other places.

My books center around the topic of pet loss grief and enable my clients to mourn their deceased animal companions. Thus, I managed to find a unique purpose for my writing. I am confident that you have something unique to offer the world, too.

Books For Your Business

If you are running a pet business, a book can be a great way to both market yourself and also offer clients additional products. It can raise awareness about your brand and products or services. Finally, it can become a product in and of itself that you can offer customers.

As a result of writing for my pet loss grief center, I now have a huge following. I have helped many people around the world. My books are unique and a direct byproduct of the business I created.

Ask Yourself:

- What your type of business is
- What topic within that business you want to address with your book
- How you can spin the book to market your business

If you sell homemade and organic pet treats, for instance, write a book about pet nutrition, why brand name treats may not be the best for our beloved companions, and how your treats are ideal for pet health and owner convenience. This offers customers something tangible—a book full of useful information—and also markets your treat products, all in one.

Passion Project

A passion project is a book that centers around a passion you have, not a business you run. For example, my passions are animals and writing, so I wrote an entire series of books about pet blogging, pet jobs, and pet authorpreneurship that you can find on Amazon (Resources).

I also write children's picture books called *The Adventures of Ms. Addie Pants* (https://amazon.com/author/wendyvandepoll). These books pay tribute to my rescue dog and the lessons she learned as she grew up. My premise for the Ms. Addie Pants series was to teach children they can believe in themselves with unaltering love, friends, and family.

In addition, I have a pen name, W. Van de Poll, for fiction, under which I write a series of cozy mysteries (https://amazon.com/author/wvandepoll). This series has a talking dog named Addie and a budding witch with animal-communicating abilities named Sarah. Both of them save the town of Witchland from environmental destruction. Writing cozy mysteries has always been a passion for me.

Does it come easy for me to write fiction? *No.* But since I am passionate about the premise behind my characters and message, I am having fun.

Your passions are areas of life you undoubtedly know a lot about and also care about. Passions in life are great sources for stories and messages that you can share with your readers.

You may also want to use your book as a way to connect with other people who share your passion. For instance, if you are a passionate dressage champion with a wall of awards, you will be able to connect with other dressage riders. Your book won't appeal to anyone outside of the dressage world, and that is okay. Your purpose here is connecting with dressage riders and imparting a message that will make a difference in their lives and competitions.

The important thing is you are writing from your heart and sharing your deep enthusiasm for animals. This alone will excite readers and influence their lives. When you write about your passion, you instill the same in others.

Your book can raise awareness about some pet-related cause, inspire people to take action, and/or help people enter a pet-related hobby of choice. Whether you are attempting to educate readers or inspire them, your book will offer them something useful that they can utilize in their own lives.

Fiction or Nonfiction?

Will your book be fiction—a story you came up with? Or will it be nonfiction—based on facts and information? Or will it even be a hybrid of the two—such as a fictional children's book that shows children how to actually take care of dogs? Your book is your creation; determine what direction you want to take with it.

Nonfiction is based on facts and information, but that does not mean it has to be a boring, dry textbook. You can offer personal anecdotes, client examples, memorable quotes, and even jokes as part of your nonfiction writing. Have fun with it. If you can present facts in an interesting way, your readers will love you all the more for it.

Fiction, similarly, does not have to be lighthearted stories about cute kittens—though we all love those, too! You can impart a powerful message through your fiction writing. By using fictional stories to relate to readers and stimulate their emotions, you create a stunning platform for delivering a realistic message. A fiction story about shelter animals can inspire readers to adopt instead of shop and to spay or neuter their pets to keep shelter populations down, for instance.

Do not let genre labels and previous books create a box that limits your creativity. If you have a unique idea that bends genres and combines fiction and nonfiction—go for it!

Wrap-Up

In this chapter, you learned how to decide what you want to write about. The action steps at the end of this chapter will also help you laser focus your project.

I presented ways to:

- Find your purpose and topic
- Discover if your book is a passion or business project
- Decide if you want to write fiction or nonfiction
- Be unique and follow your passion

Keep in mind your book has to be about something. Find out what that something is and split your ideas into groups to ensure that they are related. When you have a cluster of related ideas, you are able to find the true topic of your book and related subtopics to include. I will cover this in more detail in Chapter 3.

Find the story you want to tell. Then identify the message you want to leave with readers after they read your story. Your book can be nonfiction or fiction, a passion project or a business-related book, but it still has to have a story and message under the book's overarching topic.

In Chapter 2, you are going to learn about creating your avatar (Glossary). But before you read on, take some time with the action steps. They will help you tremendously, whether you are a first-time writer or a seasoned author who wants better results.

Action Steps

Ask yourself the questions listed in this section and write them down. If there is no answer, move to the next. Then use these notes to help shape your ideas as you continue reading this book. Remember, do not let genres or rules limit your creativity.

1. Why do I want to write a book?
2. What is my purpose?
3. What is my vision?
4. What issues do my readers have?
5. How do I want to solve those issues?
6. Is it a passion project?
7. Do I want to write fiction or nonfiction? Why?
8. Will my book serve the purpose of supporting my business?
9. Do I want my book to be purely educational?
10. Will my book change lives?

2

CREATE YOUR AVATAR

If the book is true, it will find an audience that is meant to read it.
— Wally Lamb

Are you clear about who you are writing your nonfiction or fiction book for? In my experience, if I am not clear about my audience, my writing is all over the place, self-editing is not fun, and my editor gets her red pen out with a vengeance.

It is important to create an avatar (Glossary) before you begin to write. This is a detailed description of one person who will love your book. Your avatar is like a real person—they have a name and family status. They live in a particular place and have hopes and dreams like any one of us. You write the book for them.

I promise you, this step will make your job easier when you are brainstorming, writing, and marketing your book.

Creating an avatar will:

- Help you write your book with focus and direction
- Give you a clear picture as to who you are writing for—an audience
- Direct you to appropriate marketing venues
- Laser focus your target audience—those who will buy and read your book

Keep in mind, people seek books that match the topic they are looking for and that speak to them. Particularly in the pet genres. Animal lovers will spend hours searching for the perfect book to meet their needs. When you are clear about who you are writing for, it will be easier for your potential reader to decide if your book is for them. The result—better reviews for you.

This means your book is not going to appeal to just anyone—it will appeal to a specific type of person. Thus, you must find ways to reach that particular person and convince him or her to give your book a try.

When it comes to creating an avatar, you do not need to expend too much effort thinking of every possible reader. That is too mind-boggling and confusing. Instead, develop a picture of one single person who will love your book. Give this person an identity, complete with:

- Name
- Social class
- Place to live
- Family status
- Interests

- And more

Should you ever describe your avatar to someone, he or she will be able to picture the person perfectly because you have specific details. Creating an avatar is fun and inspiring. You will be making up the perfect fictional character who absolutely loves your book.

Create Your Avatar

Start with asking yourself, "Who do I really think would love my book?"

In my case, my reader avatar was a middle-aged, educated woman who had lost her beloved dog and/or cat. Of course, in time, my avatar expanded as I did my research and developed a more concrete method for how to create my avatar. I wanted my book to appeal to someone who felt lonely after losing a close animal companion and who had little human support. I knew that type of person was out there and she would love my books.

For niche-specific books like mine, your avatar should be fairly easy and straightforward. If you are teaching people about snake handling, for instance, you know your readers will be people interested in snakes. But who is interested in snakes? "A lot of people" is the short answer. The long answer would be people who are typically daredevils, non-conformists, animal lovers, geeky types, etc.

You can make some educated guesses and then perform some research to back up your ideas. Who seems to be into snakes? Look up snake groups on Facebook and look at the profiles of members. Visit local reptile shops and get a feel for the crowd.

What About Fiction?

For fiction books, the reader avatar may seem a bit trickier. You can employ your imagination here. Who would like a horse book, for instance? Probably a pre-teenage girl or a woman who owns horses. Who would love a Christmas cat cozy? Probably a middle-aged woman who likes romance but does not read violent mysteries and who needs a cute, heart-warming distraction from the stressors of daily life.

Forming your avatar does not require exact science. You do not have to be spot-on. You are creating a "person" to appeal to for your marketing. You are developing your voice as well when you consider how to write for this person.

Why is This Important?

Creating a reader avatar is actually quite important.

For one thing, when you first get the idea for a book, you may not know how to write it. Technical, formal language may appeal to certain people, while a friendly, informal tone would appeal to others. By determining the type of person who would love your book, you can determine the type of style you should write in.

I know my readers would come from many different demographics, but I also know they are looking for compassion, support, and love—not a scientific dissertation. That helped me find a voice to match their expectations.

For my readers, if I wrote in a silly tone, I would alienate them in their moments of grief, when they needed my books the most. But if I wrote in a scientific, formal tone, I would also alienate them because they were not looking for a lecture. I had to find a voice that was compatible with their needs to make them want to keep reading.

This is going to be your first mission when creating a reader avatar. How do you write to make someone love your book? You now know your topic from Chapter 1, but you also need to find your voice and tone. It helps guide your writing and prevents you from rewriting the book later. Ask yourself, "What would this character (my reader avatar) want from this book?"

Next

A reader avatar helps you figure out how to market your book. Once the writing is done, you have to engage with readers and post on social media relating to your book. You also have to create marketing emails, a book description, and other such content that convinces people to buy the book.

The only way to get people to read the book is by making them feel the book is right for their needs. By knowing your reader avatar, you can target people with marketing that makes them think, "Yes! This is what I want!"

The reader avatar helps shape everything—the book cover design, description, and the marketing. You have to know this avatar well to both write and market. But your launch team (Chapter 13) will also have to know who your avatar is. This will help them review your book. In short, you reader avatar will drive sales.

Finally

What if you are hiring a ghostwriter to write the book for you? A ghostwriter is a viable option if you do not have the time or skills to write a book on your own. After hiring a ghostwriter, you have to ensure this writer can create the book you truly want. You have to be clear and specific in your instructions. The only way to do this is to provide the writer with an avatar that he or she can clearly understand and base the book on.

Let's Build Your Avatar

Demographics

The first half of your avatar is built upon the demographics of your reader, or the basic facts about his or her existence. You can start by determining these details:

- Gender
- Age
- Family status
- Marital status
- Income
- Career
- Amount of spare time
- Where he or she lives
- Whether he or she lives in an apartment or house

Psychographics

The second half relates to psychographics, or your reader's interests, values, and needs. This is the psychology of your reader that drives him or her to buy your book. Ask yourself these things:

1. What does my reader value?
2. What does my reader like?
3. What does he or she dislike?
4. What is he or she looking for in a book?
5. What is his or her biggest fear?
6. Favorite book, music, and movie?
7. What are his or her hobbies?
8. What pet does he or she share life with?
9. What does he or she want for this pet?
10. How does this person want to feel?
11. How would this person describe himself/herself?
12. What are his or her dreams and aspirations?
13. What are some of his or her habits?
14. How does this person feel about spending money on books? (This is important for setting a price and convincing the reader that the price on the book is worthwhile.)
15. How often does he or she read? (This helps you determine the length of the book and tone.)

Next

As you build your avatar, ask the above questions and jot down short, simple answers. Maybe find a picture online of some person who matches this avatar. As you answer the questions, you start to build a robust picture in your mind. To ensure you do not lose this picture, be sure to write it down and create at least five paragraphs describing this fictitious person.

Once you have built an avatar from these answers, read it to someone. See if the person can picture your reader based on this avatar. If someone else can picture a person based on your avatar, then you know that you have a strong one that you can reliably build a book around. You want to make sure other people can picture this avatar simply because you will be sharing your avatar with your launch team later on.

Sample Avatar

Here is a sample avatar for a snake handling book.

Ethan is a thirty-seven-year-old motorcycle mechanic and detailer. He owns his own business and is married with no children. He is heavily tattooed and has a free spirit.

He lives in a rented house with his wife and two dogs. He drives a standard truck that he fixed up himself and also has two motorcycles. He spends his weekends riding, taking long trips with his wife, and taking his dogs on long walks. His family often hosts large barbecues where lots of friends get together on weekends, listen to rock, drink beer, and let their dogs play together. While he is not rich, he is also sure to designate money for the things he enjoys.

People think he is tough, but he is a teddy bear at heart. Animals are his main love in life, and he will do anything for his dogs. His greatest fear is doing something wrong as a pet lover. To rectify this fear, he likes to be informed and spend money on books that educate him. He prefers an informal tone he can relate to, but he also appreciates clear, concise, accurate information.

Now Ethan wants to make his dream of owning a snake come true. He is ready to get a snake and everything he needs for the reptile to be happy, but he wants to learn about caring for snakes first. He is looking for a solid guide to inform him.

Ethan is interested in getting an ebook he can read on his phone before bed because he is too busy to read at any other time. He is willing to spend a decent amount of money on an ebook, but he has to be sure the ebook he gets will deliver all of the information that he needs. He will be comparing a few in order to select the best one. His wife will want to read the book, too, because she shares his desire to get a snake and provide the best care for it.

You want to write a book that Ethan would like. Full of useful information, loving and compassionate toward animals, informal and relatable, perhaps some humor and a laid-back vibe. You want to offer a decent price (no more than $5.99) and stand out from the competition by offering more or better information than other books on the same topic. Your love of snakes will make Ethan like your book more because he will feel like he can relate to you.

Dear Avatar

In Chapter 8, I am going to share with you in more detail the different ways in which to write a rough draft. However, before I share those methods with you, keep in mind this exercise.

I use this exercise for every chapter in my books. I start by writing the chapter as a letter to my avatar. First, I pose a question according to my avatar profile, mind mapping, and outline. Then I write my letter to my avatar in a way that will answer that question and continue with the chapter from there. When I get to the self-editing phase (Chapter 9) I clean up the draft by removing their name and any reference that would confuse my readers.

My writing clients love this exercise, whether they are writing nonfiction or fiction pet books. It can make your writing journey personal, fun, and productive. Here are some examples:

Nonfiction

Chapter 1: What is Normal Grief?

Dear Sally (my avatar for my pet loss grief nonfiction),

Are people telling you that your feelings are crazy? Sally, I have heard comments from people who do not understand the emotions of pet loss grief that are hurtful. Let me help you by outlining the normal feelings of grief.

Chapter 1: Courage and Inspiration (*Pet Blogging 101*)

Dear Laura (my avatar for The Pet Biz Series),

So you want to start a pet blog? Do you know where to begin? Do not worry, Laura, if you are nervous about this venture. I was, too, when I first started writing blog articles. It takes courage to put yourself out there, but the rewards are phenomenal!

Fiction

Chapter 1:

Dear Tina (my avatar for The Spellbound Paranormal Cozy Mystery Witch Series),

Would you like to meet Sarah and Addie? Would you like to know what they are getting themselves into? Please let me introduce Sarah Spellwood and her dog, Addie. The thing is—whenever people heard her last name, Sarah would almost instantly raise her hand and say that, yes, she was related to that famous witch, Lativia Spellwood. But despite her last name, she did not believe in witches—or faerie folk, for that matter.

Wrap-Up

An avatar is a crucial piece of information about how to shape your book and market it. Your book can appeal to many people, but base it on one person who could really use the information or enjoy your story. Your tone should match what this person would appreciate. You can perform research to help you find your reader avatar.

Keep in mind, no one will bother to buy it unless they get a good sense it will satisfy their needs. This is why creating your pet-loving avatar will help you write a great book and help you with marketing later (Chapter 15 and 16).

Please do not be concerned if you know nothing about marketing. I will teach you about the basics on how to market your book and find a knowledgeable team in Section III. All you have to do now is develop your reader avatar. This exercise helps you match your book to the ideal person who will buy your book.

Before you go to Chapter 3, where you will learn about taking your ideas and putting them down on paper, check out the action steps for this chapter. Then proceed to discover how mind mapping is a great way to get your ideas down and organized.

Action Steps

1. Answer the demographic questions in this chapter.
2. The psychographic questions in this chapter are also important—do not skip.
3. Write the avatar's characteristics down in detail.
4. Research if necessary. Social media groups, local pet clubs, and/or shops are great for this!
5. Get a picture of the person who would like your book in your mind.
6. If you have clients, consider doing some polls to get an idea of their needs.
7. Get to know your avatar well—you will be "talking to them" in the next two sections in this book.
8. Read your creation to a friend. Can he or she picture this person?
9. Overall, figure out what this person wants and consider this with your mind mapping efforts.

3

MIND MAPPING TECHNIQUES

'Let's put on our thinking caps and see if we cannot have an idea,' said Cricket, passing the caps around.
— Anna Rose Wright, *Whirligig House*

Do you have a ton of ideas in your head, and are you having difficulty putting your first word on paper? My solution—stop trying to write your book, now! Instead, consider a mind map.

Mind mapping (Glossary) is the process of getting your mind's thoughts onto paper and organizing them. Then you can use the mind maps to outline (Chapter 4) your manuscript. When you have a ton of ideas in your head, they can seem convoluted, messy, and disjointed. But when you create a graphical representation of these ideas, they start to make sense.

The great thing about mind maps is you can figure out how to develop, manipulate, pattern, and order your ideas. This will help you when you are outlining and writing your first draft for your avatar (Chapter 2).

While reading is a visual activity, your brain processes the written word quite differently from a picture. It is harder to organize blocks of text or sentence fragments into a cohesive whole when they are not down on paper. That is why you use a mind map to make your ideas visual.

There are many different forms of mind maps. You can certainly find one that works for you. I use different techniques—depending on the book. For example: I use different mind maps for fiction and nonfiction. And I have different techniques for my pet loss books and for this series (The Pet Biz Series).

The one aspect they all share is how they make complicated ideas simple. They quiet and organize the convolution of ideas in your head. And they present information in an accessible manner.

Let's take a look at some of the different mind mapping options you have to help you create a stellar book for pet lovers and/or professionals.

When to Use a Mind Map

You will want to use a mind map for a variety of tasks within the process of writing your nonfiction and/or fiction manuscript. For example:

1. Creating a character for fiction: You want to figure out who the character is, details of the character's life, things that will happen to the character in the story, and how the character relates to other characters. This helps you remember details, since consistency is key in any book.

2. Organizing your plot for fiction: You have a rough idea of where you want the book to go, but you need to connect the dots and determine everything that happens. As you get ideas for the plot, you can sort them into beginning, ending, and middle. You can also keep track of events and maintain consistency if you are using an alternate timeline—something other than chronological where keeping track of events can be difficult.

3. Summarizing all crucial information for nonfiction: You want to be sure to cover many useful topics in your nonfiction pet book, but what if you forget one or two ideas while you are writing? It is known to happen! Also, what if you cannot figure out where to place a point or subtopic in the overall scheme of the book? A mind map can help you figure out how ideas relate and where each idea fits in the book.

4. Getting ideas down: You have tons of ideas—you want to get them down before you forget any of them. You will want to make sense of these ideas and remove the ones that do not fit into the manuscript. A mind map will help you find how ideas relate to each other in order to organize them into a book form.

5. Working out a problem: You want to show readers how to do something or you want something to happen in your fiction plot, but you cannot figure out how to present your story. A mind map can help you brainstorm a variety of ideas and test them. Then you can narrow your options down to the best one.

6. Organizing research: As you research a topic, you find new things to include in your manuscript. You want to save those facts for later when you are ready to write about them.

Types of Mind Maps

A Tree Map

These are more useful for mapping out nonfiction.

Step One: With a tree map, you want to start with a piece of blank paper and at least three colored pens. The trunk of the tree is your basic idea, or the main subject of the book.

Start by writing your basic idea vertically down the center of the paper and draw some lines around it to form a tree trunk. You can use one color for your core subject. For instance, my book might be about overcoming grief after pet loss—that is my trunk. I write it vertically, and it forms a tree trunk in red pen.

Step Two: Start writing your main ideas that connect to your overall basic idea as the branches in the second color. These are the points you will touch on within your book—no exceptions.

I generally draw a thick, curvy line to represent each branch and then write the idea in black pen. Generally, I let each connecting idea represent one chapter. My branches might include how children grieve, how to have a pet funeral, how to memorialize your pet, normal aspects of the grieving process, etc. A chapter will center around each branch.

Step 3: For each connecting idea or branch, you want to write down different subtopics. Such as how you plan to present the idea or related smaller subtopics that you plan to write about. These will be in the third color.

Under the branch on how children grieve, I would draw

several tinier branches shooting off the big one in blue, including subtopics like "Explaining Death to a Child," "Emotional Support," and "Activities Your Child Can Do." Often, these become subchapters or separate sections within the book, or I may work them all together underneath the same chapter. As long as I get my ideas down and they are directed toward the needs of my avatar (Chapter 2), I am content—because I know I'm not missing anything.

Example

A book about house-training a puppy would have *house-training puppies* as the trunk. Then each branch would be a *chapter*, and each offshoot from the branch is a *subtopic within the chapter*. For example:

- Branch 1 or Chapter 1 - House-Training Methods
- Branch 2 or Chapter 2 - Rewards and Positive Reinforcement
- Branch 3 or Chapter 3 - How to Avoid Negative Reinforcement
- Branch 4 or Chapter 4 - Reading Your Puppy's Cues, etc.

Off of each branch are offshoots with *subtopics*, such as:

- Offshoot for Branch 1 or subtopic - Types of Training Tools
- Offshoot for Branch 2 or subtopic - Types of Treats to Give a Puppy for Going Outside
- Offshoot for Branch 3 or subtopic - What Words to Choose for Training

- Offshoot for Branch 4 or subtopic - Body Language, Tail Positioning, Facial Expressions

As you get new ideas, find the branches and offshoots (subtopics) where you can add them. When you do this exercise, you will never forget an idea, and you can organize the information for nonfiction in a useful way. If words do not work for you, you can use images to make the mind map even more visual and striking.

Your tree map can get quite huge as you develop ideas. You can prune it at any time to get rid of ideas that do not fit into the book or offer much significance to your topic or avatar.

Maybe, as you write and research, you realize some ideas are beyond the scope of your book and need to be pruned. Be flexible and open to cutting out ideas to keep your book reasonable and on topic.

Thought Bubbles and Flow Charts

These can be used for both fiction and nonfiction.

When I have tons of ideas, I like to write them down as they come to me. Thought bubbles and flow charts can be helpful when you want to get your ideas or plot points down fast.

When this happens, I write my idea in different colored markers on a whiteboard in my writing space. The different colors help me tell them apart. When my ideas are all down on the whiteboard, I'm ready to get organized.

Then: I draw circles around each idea, plot point, or chapter to create a bubble and use lines to connect bubbles that relate to each other. In time, I can keep drawing lines to create a sort of flow chart, where one idea flows into the next or one events flows into the next to create a sequence.

Next: When I have my flow chart, I then take that information and enter it into an outline format. I can now see the placement and relation of ideas or plot points so I know where to stick them in the outline.

Example - Nonfiction

Let's go back to the example of my pet loss grief book. I might have a dozen ideas about how to help children grieve pet loss. I write them all down where they fit on the board. Then I see how important it is to explain how children grieve and express their grief. I choose this to be the central idea that needs to be explained before I write anything else. I circle the central idea and start the entire flow chart from that point.

From there, I draw a line to the next subtopic, how to talk to children about grief and explain death. Then I draw another line connecting to activities children can do to mourn and grieve pet loss.

Now, in my outline, I can start the chapter on children and pet grief with the subtopic about how children perceive loss and express grief. The next section is about talking to children about death and grief. After that, I place the subtopic about activities. And now I have an outline for the whole chapter.

Example – Fiction

A fiction example is a bit more difficult to give because as writers we all have different preferences and personalities. However, when you have a flow chart or your road map calculated it can make your job so much easier. Here is a condensed example of my flow chart for my cozy mystery fiction series.

1. Ordinary world: Sarah Spellwood is a former attorney from New York City finding herself in a small New England town full of paranormal people and a talking dog.

2. Inciting incident: Sarah's mentor is killed and it completely changes her life.

3. Setting: Witchland, New Hampshire.

4. Identify main character's greatest fear: Sarah is afraid of the paranormal.

5. Identify main character's happiest moment: Sarah gets to see Michael again.

6. Main character's external goal: To save the town of Witchland and all it's inhabitants.

7. Main character's internal goal: To figure out her purpose.

8. Obstacles– what or who gets in the way of her achieving her goal: The bad guys and Madras.

9. What will happen if the main character doesn't get what she wants: Witchland, New Hampshire will be destroyed.

10. The quest. The journey your character takes to find her new ordinary world: Sarah turns to learning environmental and paranormal law. She also learns about her spirit animals that help save Witchland.

11. The fork in the road. Your character has to choose which way to go. Each path/decision has consequences: Sarah has to

make a choice whether to believe in her abilities as an animal communicator, witch, and psychic.

12. The black moment. This is when everything that can go wrong does. The character's worst fear happens: Witchland is on the verge of complete destruction.

13. The climax. The ultimate point of tension in the story: The real killer is revealed.

14. The aha moment. That moment when your character discovers something internal about himself. Or when he realizes the lie he thought was the truth, was really a lie: When Sarah is comfortable with her new changes and sees the utility in them for her to forge on.

15. The happily-ever-after–or not: Sarah gets closer to becoming content with her new life on many levels.

This is a brief example of what I do for my entire book as a whole and for each chapter. When I have this flow chart completed my mind map can easily be made into an outline (Chapter 4).

Post-It Notes

These can be used for both fiction and nonfiction.

Another mind mapping technique is to purchase a large poster board and a collection of differently colored Post-it notes. Or find a large wall in your home or writing space.

Example - Nonfiction

1. Write your central idea on one note and stick it in the center of the board.

2. You can start working outward with other notes containing other ideas.

3. When you have an idea, jot it down on a note and stick it to the board in the appropriate place.

4. I usually like to color-code my notes. Connecting ideas or sub-plots to the central idea will be green, while ideas I will write about under each connecting idea are pink.

5. Sometimes you won't know if an idea is worthy of its own chapter or simply a subtopic, so do not worry too much about color-coding in the beginning. You can always rewrite the notes in the proper color when you get organized later on.

6. When you have your ideas down, you can then rearrange the Post-it notes in order of importance. Change the colors if you must.

With Post-it notes, the central idea stays in the center and is surrounded by important supporting ideas worthy of their own chapters or at least some emphasis. Further out are the supporting ideas that go into each chapter. You can use strings and thumbtacks to link ideas with lines.

Example – Fiction

Again, either get a large board or designate a few walls in your writing studio to create your mind map. I have a few fiction walls going at once because I have so many ideas going for my series.

1. Write your main idea or working title (Glossary) down on a Post-it and stick it in the center of the board.

2. As you work outward you will have each chapter noted.

3. Under each chapter you will have the main scene for each chapter.

4. Under each main scene you could note a particular incident.

5. I find it equally as helpful to include a Post-it for each character I am including in my story and their point-of-view.

Using Post-it notes for fictions can be as creative as you want. I gave you a condensed example of what I do to get me going. I branch off from this basic idea as my story develops.

Computer Software

Nonfiction books are usually not terribly complicated to mind map and outline. I love to make my maps messy and organize them once my thoughts are documented. The act of using my hands and creating a beautiful mind map satisfies my creative personality.

But fiction novels can get quite complex, and you have a lot to keep track of. The more convoluted your plot is, the more you should consider using a computer software to mind map your ideas.

There are several software options for brainstorming and mind mapping. Scapple (Resources) is one of them. Personally, I still love the activity of using Post-its, markers, and the creative wall in my writing studio. But for those of you who rather use computer software, many of my authorpreneur friends love Scapple for fiction.

Wrap-Up

Mind mapping is a critical step to getting organized and making your ideas clear. Once you organize your ideas, it will be easy to form an outline (Chapter 4). By using one of the mind mapping techniques I presented, you will never forget an idea, and you will stop feeling lost about how to get started with your writing.

Consider mind mapping to be part of the creative process—instead of a dreaded exercise. It takes patience to write a book, and the more time you spend with preparation, the better your rough draft (Chapter 8) will be.

In the next chapter, you will learn how to outline your manuscript from your mind map. It is a short chapter, but necessary if you are writing your first book. Remember to do all the action steps before you go on so outlining is less of a challenge.

Action Steps

1. Have the idea for your topic well established (Chapter 1).
2. Develop your avatar from Chapter 2 before you get started with mind mapping.
3. Purchase the necessary supplies. Markers, paper, Post-its, etc.
4. Establish a place in your writing studio, home, etc., where your mind map is a "permanent fixture" (i.e., you do not have to move it until you are done with your writing).

5. Play with the methods presented in this chapter and find one that works for you.
6. Choose the best method of mind mapping for your needs.
7. Start mind mapping your ideas with your chosen method or a mixture of methods.
8. Have fun—this is part of the creativity of writing a book.

4

OUTLINING YOUR MANUSCRIPT

The work is always accomplished one word at a time.
—*Stephen King*

What is an outline, and why do you need one? Before you get started writing, it is important to organize the information in your visual mind map into a usable written outline. Your outline is the basic plan and flow of your topic and/or story. It is a skeleton of your manuscript and your blueprint to finally use when you start writing.

I like to think of my nonfiction outlines as a journey to create a comprehensive guide for my avatar. And in fiction, my outlines are adventures to deepen my creative outlet to entertain my avatar.

Nonfiction

My outlines for nonfiction are not too fancy. Mainly, I want to get my mind map organized in chapters that focus on the needs of my avatar. Here is what I include:

1. I start with my title—what I call a "Working Title" (Glossary)—because often a great title does not come to me until I have finished the book. A working title is the basic name of your book that sums up the book's theme and central idea. It can be boring and clunky—what matters is it states what the book is about. Do not worry about it for now.

2. Next, I always write "introduction," since every book needs an introduction. Here you may also want to include additional things such as forewords or notes.

3. After that, I write each chapter number and the basic topic of the chapter. Again, I do not stress about catchy names unless I have one in mind already. Make sure the topic of the chapter is clear by the name.

4. I also include a conclusion or afterword at the end. Every book needs to be concluded nicely—with its points summarized for the reader. Of course, I should add, a conclusion and an introduction are not always necessary in fiction books.

5. When I have my chapters down, I go back to Chapter 1 and start outlining the information and ideas I want to include in that chapter. Looking at my mind map, I know what will go into Chapter 1—I write those ideas down. I bold the ones that will become subheadings, or separate sections. I leave the supporting ideas under these subheadings alone for now until I know what precisely to do with them later.

This is a basic outline. I now have a clear guideline for writing my book. I start at the beginning and work my way through, completing subsections as I go. I always save my introduction and conclusion for last.

Fiction

When I outline fiction, I go into great detail and describe what happens in each chapter. An outline in fiction can take me at least three to six weeks. You do not have to do an outline if your mind does not work in this way, but I have found creating a detailed outline for fiction helps me when the actual writing takes place. Writer's block (Glossary) isn't something I have to deal with because I spent time organizing and fleshing out my ideas and plot points.

Outlining for fiction is very detailed and beyond the scope of this book, but here is a list of what I include in my fiction outlines. My goal for this chapter is to give you an idea of what goes into a basic outline.

Step 1: Setting the Stage

The first step is to come up with your premise (Glossary). Your premise is where you answer the questions, *What if? What is expected? What is unexpected?* Write your premise in two sentences.

For example: (Your character) must (do something) to (story goal) or else (reason why your avatar should be concerned).

Character Profiles: I will cover this more in Chapter 5. But right now, you should have a clear idea of who all your characters are before you start outlining your fiction manuscript. Basically, understand his or her motives, relationships, desires, traits, etc.

Think About the Big Picture: How is your story going to begin and end? What is the central conflict and the major turning point? What happens between these points?

For example, consider the:

- Beginning of your story

- First inciting incident

- Rising action

- Falling action

- Resolution

Step 2: Organize Your Scenes

These are the questions you can ask as you create the scenes in your manuscript:

Decide how you will:

- Organize the scenes so they flow and build upon your premise

- Introduce your characters

- Connect the scenes to the big picture of your story (See Setting the Stage)

Step 3: Troubleshooting Issues

When writing fiction, your first draft with your outline isn't going to be perfect, but its purpose is to prevent you from running into issues while you are writing.

Some common examples:

- A scene has an undeveloped idea

- There is no connection between two scenes

- A particular scene makes no sense and does not fit

- A plot hole (Glossary) is revealed

Wrap-Up

Whether you are writing nonfiction or fiction animal books, outlines are a great way to keep your thoughts organized. When you spend time with an outline, you will avoid future issues with your manuscript.

Creating an outline happens directly after mind mapping. This is a simple step, crucial for guiding your writing because you know what to write about and when. You can build your writing schedule, covered in Chapter 6, around this outline.

Always consider your avatar and mind map when creating your outline. This consideration will help you with your writing later on. Although you might want to skip this part—please do not. Honestly, like everything else I presented to you so far, outlining will help you with writing your rough draft.

As promised, in the next chapter, I am going to help you develop your character profiles. When you know your characters well, you will have solutions if an issue arises. Before you go to Chapter 5, please check out the action steps for this chapter.

Action Steps

1. Have your avatar created and mind map completed.
2. Do additional research for outlining your nonfiction or fiction book.
3. For nonfiction and fiction, set a working title for your manuscript.
4. If you are writing nonfiction, consider the topic and subtopic for all chapters.
5. Do not forget to set the stage, organize your scenes, and troubleshoot your outline with fiction.
6. When writing fiction, have a well-thought-out outline—beginning, first inciting incident, rising action, falling action, and resolution.

5

CHARACTER PROFILES FOR FICTION

*Character is like a tree, and reputation is like its shadow. The
shadow is what we think of it;
the tree is the real thing.
—Abraham Lincoln*

Do you know the characters in your story? When writing fiction, you must know your characters well. Character development is an enjoyable step in the writing process. Why? Because you can create any personality you want. When creating a character profile (Glossary), you need to understand his or her motives, relationships, and traits as they fit into your story.

For each character:

- Outline who the character is
- What he or she does in the book
- How he or she relates to other characters

Always save these profiles in case you need them later. Do not be afraid to edit them as needed. When I create character profiles, I keep them all handy while writing. This way, I can refer to them throughout the writing process and change them if necessary. When I get new ideas, I can add them to a particular character's profile. Like real people, characters grow and evolve.

I write each character profile in a separate document and save them under the same file titled "Characters for [enter name of story]." If you organize yourself in this way, you can easily retrieve the information when you need it.

Furthermore, you can save each profile and use characters later on for other stories. Maybe you create a great character, but she does not fit into the story you are writing now. You can save her for a later story where she is better suited. Or maybe you want to write a sequel or prequel and you need to read a character's profile to get reacquainted. Never get rid of character profiles!

Steps to Create Your Character Profile

First: I always start with the bare bones. I make up a name, age, and a brief description of the character's appearance. I'm not much of an artist, so I usually write the description, but if you feel like drawing the character or even using a photo of someone who resembles the character, go for it!

The more visual the better. You want to be able to picture your character perfectly in your mind's eye. But I also describe the character's basic personality for a guide on how to shape dialogue and make the character react to the other characters.

Second: I list how the character relates to everyone. Is he or she cousins with someone in the story? Who is he or she dating? How does he or she know the main character? Sometimes, it is helpful to create family trees or flow charts showing how the character relates to the other characters.

Third: I create a backstory (Glossary). The backstory does not have to be long or detailed, but it needs to explain why a character does what he or she does, and it needs to provide relevant information to the story. A backstory might include how the character's father left when he was young, creating self-esteem issues and trust issues for the character.

Fourth: I determine the character's place in the story and ask:

Is he or she the main character, a supporting character, an antagonist (a villain), or the protagonist (the hero)? You will also want to determine how much importance the character has to the overall story and how much you should focus on him or her.

I summarize this information briefly. Remember, this profile is flexible, and the character's relevance in the story can change. Sometimes I come up with awesome characters who do not fit into the story. I have to cut them out, as much as I hate doing so. Other times, insignificant characters suddenly have great uses in the story—I then make them more important.

Finally: Last but not least, I figure out a rough outline of what happens to the character throughout the story. From beginning to end, I show how the character plays into the overall story. I want to summarize what the character does, feels, and says. Then I want to show how the character is affected by the whole story.

Example

Let's say you have a character named Susie. She is short, about thirty-five, with short brown hair and two Afghan hounds. Susie is jealous, competitive, and domineering, but she also loves to help, and she has a special place in her heart for animals.

Susie can be rude and abrasive, but her occasional acts of kindness betray she is a good person at heart.

Now I create her backstory. Susie grew up with a critical mother, which is why she is competitive and always has to win. There is a strong rivalry between her and the main character, as they both compete with their dogs. Susie envies the main character's trophies.

Susie is officially the antagonist to the main character, and she is going to be the villain of the story, but you also want to make people sympathize with her because she's not an evil person at heart. She is a cousin to the main character, and they have been in competition since they were kids.

Susie's role in the plot is to sabotage the main character's dog show so she will win. The main character has to find out what Susie did, confront her, and somehow resolve the conflict.

You could write down things like:

- What Susie does throughout the story
- Some flashbacks and dialogue to show how the main character and Susie have been competing with each other for years
- A few acts of kindness on Susie's part

- Some scenes with vulnerability where Susie cries about her critical mother's cruel words to make readers sympathize with her more
- A happy ending where Susie finds peace with herself and makes up with the main character

Now you have a completed character profile for Susie.

Wrap-Up

Your characters are a vital piece to writing your fiction book. They can make your book exciting or boring. It is crucial to have a clear idea of who they are before you start outlining—how they got to a certain point in their life, how they think, their desires, goals, and wishes.

A character profile gives you a focal point for writing. They can help you get your creativity flowing. You can test them out in different scenes to determine if they are influential and/or necessary. You can even *talk* to them and find out their secrets to make your story more interesting.

There is a lot to consider when developing your characters. Interview them by asking pertinent questions about who they are, what they like, life experiences, political views, etc. Give your imagination the freedom to write down every idea your character wants you to know.

You have now completed Section I: Get Ready to Write. You figured out what you want to write about, created your avatar, designed your mind map, outlined your manuscript, and created character profiles for writing fiction (if that is your choice).

After you do the action steps for this chapter, go to Section II: Ready. Set. Write. I will show you how to allocate time for your writing, ways to stay motivated, how to write your rough draft, and more.

Action Steps

1. Make a list of all your characters.
2. Give each character a separate file or piece of paper.
3. Ask them as many questions as you can possibly think of: name, age, job, salary, enemies, lives with, fights with, outlook on life, do they like themselves, personal demons, etc.
4. Figure out how your character relates to others.
5. Determine where your character fits into the story.
6. Always figure out and document the backstory of your character.
7. Establish what happens to your character in the story.

SECTION II

READY. SET. WRITE.

Are you ready to get writing? Do you have your avatar, mind map, and outline done? Let's get started with your writing journey!

Maybe writing isn't fun for you yet, but it is really enjoyable once you get down to it. Whether you are a seasoned writer or a newbie, writing is a mentally complex, enriching, and entertaining experience.

There will be times where you:

- Feel stuck or cannot concentrate
- Cannot think of the right word and want to hurl your computer across the room
- Want to be doing something else instead of writing
- Cannot sleep because the ideas keep running through your head

You will find certain parts of writing you despise and parts you want to ignore. But overall, I hope you will love your writing journey just like I, and many of my clients, do.

If you are like some writers, procrastination is the worst part of writing. However, once you actually sit down to write, it can come easily. I have many useful tips in this section to help you with your writing goals.

When you accomplish your writing goals, your sense of pride and accomplishment will astound you. In this section, I will show you how to overcome procrastination, gain inspiration, work through the hard parts, and get your book ready for editing.

Are you ready? Do not put it off any longer. It is time you get your thoughts out into the world. Ready. Set. Write.

6

MAKE TIME FOR WRITING EVERY DAY

The way to write a book is the application of the seat of one's pants to the seat of one's chair.
—*J.B. Priestley*

Do you have a bunch of excuses to keep you from writing? Probably one of the biggest impediments you will face as a writer is getting over the excuses that keep you from being productive.

Your intentions are probably good. You plan on writing every morning, but sometimes life takes over. Before you know it, it's bedtime. You say you will start writing tomorrow. Tomorrow comes, and you have to do your grocery shopping. Pretty soon, six months have passed, and you only have a few sentences done.

The truth is—writing does not happen by itself. I know this seems obvious now, but trust me, the longer you put off writing, the longer it will take you to self-publish. If you are not careful, you will miss a deadline—or worse, give up on writing your book altogether. To actually finish your book, you absolutely must work on it every day and have a plan you follow.

That does not mean you have to finish a chapter a day. You do not even need to finish a whole page. As long as you work on the book a bit each day, you will see the bits add up until the book is complete.

The Benefit

This also keeps your ideas fresh in your mind. You get more inspired as you write—a process called momentum. Momentum comes from the work you have done thus far. It then builds upon itself and propels you forward. Your manuscript starts to come together, and before you know it, your rough draft is complete (Chapter 8).

As you get started, plan and pick a time each day to write. It could be ten minutes before your shift or your yoga class. It could be twenty minutes before you go to bed. As long as you work each day, you will get the book done!

Where Will you Find the Time?

With twenty-four hours in a day and a lot of those hours spent asleep, at work, fixing dinner, playing with your pets, and spending time with family—you may wonder how you can possibly make time for writing. After all, writing takes concentration, and it is quite time-consuming. You cannot exactly multitask while writing your book.

But I assure you—you do have time in the day. You have to

look at how you divvy up your activities. How many hours you actually spend in front of the television, scrolling through Facebook, or any other activity that isn't actually important.

One time, I actually measured myself and realized I was wasting a good hour and a half a day—time I could have been using to write! When I started setting aside an hour and a half a day to write thereafter, I found I did not feel the time crunch. I did not miss idly wasting my time, either.

Who knew I was wasting time—I never checked myself before. My first piece of advice is to look at how much time each day you spend on Facebook, playing solitaire, and/or searching the Internet for *nothing*. You may be surprised to see you actually do have time to write every day.

What I Tell my Clients

- Set a timer on your phone and measure yourself as you engage in different activities, like social media or napping
- Multiply the hours of your favorite television shows by how many times you watch them each week
- List the things you do every day, then weed out the things you do not actually enjoy or gain any benefit from

You will quickly find you do many things you do not need to do—thus wasting time where you could be writing.

When it comes to writing a book, you have to budget your time a bit differently. Do not worry—this does not have to be permanent. You can get back to binging on your favorite shows in a few months. For now, you are committing to a worthwhile pursuit, making a dream come true. It is worth the new time budget.

Finding the Right Time for You to Write

Most writers I have worked with have different times of day when they write best. Some people write late into the night—gaining inspiration by the solitude of darkness. Others wake up early, and their first task is to write. Yet others can write indiscriminately at any time of day.

To get a sense for when you write best, think of when you tend to have the most energy to tackle projects. Do you stay up till 2:00 a.m. making crafts? Then you might be a night owl writer. Do you wake up early feeling refreshed and energized? Then you might be a morning writer.

But if you have never written before, then you cannot know for sure when you write best until you actually try it.

A Writing Schedule For Champions

I prefer to assess what I must do for a book and then break up tasks and schedule them over time. When I plan in this way, I feel less overwhelmed and more eager to work. I also cannot put off the parts of the book I dislike doing—I have a schedule I cannot stray from. This enables me to meet deadlines and get things done. I urge you to try a schedule, too.

My Schedule For This Book

This is the process I have followed for most of my books. Your schedule can change depending if you are writing nonfiction, fiction, children's books, etc. Take my suggestions and figure out what works for you.

1. I knew I wanted to write sixteen chapters.
2. I gave myself three days for each chapter.
3. One day was for research, and two days were for writing without editing.
4. After my first draft was done, I started self-editing.
5. After four self-edits, I sent it to my editor.
6. When it came back, I made the changes and sent it to my proofreader.
7. When she finished, my beta readers (Glossary) read and critiqued it.
8. I then went to the next steps, which I will share with you in Section III.

As I suggested in Chapter 2, start by developing your avatar after you know your topic (Chapter 1), then start mind mapping (Chapter 3) and building a basic outline (Chapters 4 and 5). Then break it into chapters and determine their approximate length from your mind mapping. Guestimate how much time each chapter will take.

Make sure you set a date when you plan to finish your first draft. Some plan on three months or less. I did less than three months for most of my nonfiction books. For my fiction, it takes me longer.

Deadlines

You do not have to meet these deadlines exactly, but now you have incentive and guidance for getting the rough draft finished. As you get a sense for how fast you write, you can then adjust your timelines to be more realistic.

Please do not beat yourself up for not meeting a deadline—but also take the deadlines seriously and try to meet them to motivate yourself, which I will talk about more in the next chapter.

A Note About Research

Researching your material is a good thing, but I have found with my clients, research can easily become an excuse not to write. This is why I only allow myself one day for researching each chapter for my first draft. If I find I need more, I make a note to myself to continue research during my self-editing period.

Be honest with yourself when conducting your research. Do you really need a week of research before you start a new chapter or section? Or do you find you write better by doing all the research before you start work?

Whether you are writing nonfiction or fiction, figure out the way you want to research and how to do it. You might need more time and flexibility if you are interviewing people or traveling for research, for example. Be open to last-minute changes and take your time. This research process should not be overly stressful, or you will not want to do it.

Remember to catch yourself if your research is a form of procrastination.

Self-Editing Before You Are Finished

One of the best pieces of advice I got from Chandler Bolt, founder of the Self-Publishing School (Resources), was to *not* edit as I write. Prior to learning this, I wasn't getting my manuscript done—because I edited each sentence after I wrote it. And of course, I hated it.

When I changed my habit and wrote without reading or editing a word until I was done with my rough draft (Chapter 9), it was then I became a successful best-selling author.

Some people do prefer to self-edit at the end of each writing session, some at the end of each chapter, others at the end of each sentence or paragraph. If this is your preference, and it works for you, then do it. But always adhere to a schedule as best you can, and do not use self-editing as a method of procrastination or not getting your book done.

Your set schedule is your guide to the successful end of writing your manuscript. It helps you create a flow that writers must enter to create unimpeded. However, be flexible and change the schedule as you must. Things can, and do, happen. Please do not stress out about missing a deadline or changing the order of your writing process.

Keep a Strong Writing Schedule

Now you know why it is important to set aside time each day to write—with no exceptions. This schedule will help you complete each step of the writing process. But how do you create the discipline necessary to make yourself adhere to these habits? Not everyone has a natural ability to write in this regimented fashion.

In this regard, I compare writing to exercising. Once you get in the habit, you find it easy to write every day and follow your schedule. It becomes a reliable part of your routine you do without question. But until you have this habit and routine, you will have to force yourself to write each day. This can be particularly challenging when you struggle with procrastination.

Here are some tips to help develop discipline for writing and make your writing schedule a habit:

1. Get enough sleep. When you are well rested, your mind is sharper. That is obviously helpful for this intellectual pursuit.
2. Reading is crucial for any writer. Reading teaches you how to write, how to express ideas, how to get imagery across. You may also need to read for research. Set aside time to read each day. It does not matter what you read—just read something!
3. After reading, do your writing. Does not matter for how long, as long as you write each day.
4. Wake up, go to bed, and eat at the same times—develop a solid routine for your day. Consistency helps you develop a practice where you can fit your writing time in neatly.
5. Make your life more about writing. This means you create an immersive experience for yourself. Read blogs and articles about writing, join writer's clubs

and social media groups, take writing challenges, and attend seminars or courses on writing. Writer's retreats are also great for getting away from the demands of daily life. I even participate in a daily email word challenge called "Word of the Day" (Resources). All of these activities motivate you, remind you to write, and make you think about writing.

6. Reward yourself when you finish writing each day. Most people never even sit down and write. Take some time to pamper yourself or reward yourself in some manner. You certainly deserve it!

7. Do not worry about being perfect (Chapter 8). Focusing on fixing every little typo while you write is aggravating and distracting from your actual inspiration and content. You can forget great ideas for how to phrase something or what to write next if you go back to fix a small detail. Save all of that for self-editing, your editor, and professional proofreader. I always say just write—even if it is an incoherent mess!

8. Do not worry about readers. Worrying about how you will get five hundred readers or whether or not people will like your book is a surefire way to deaden your inspiration and confidence. You really cannot know if your book will be received well. The suspense and insecurity about readership is an inevitable facet of being a writer. Focus on writing for now and worry about readers later. Do not let insecurity kill your creativity and stall your progress. And do not worry about something you cannot know for certain or control.

9. Set a daily word count when you get familiar with your writing speed and ability. Aim for a thousand words, for example. If you can comfortably write five hundred per day, set that as your minimum—but challenge yourself by trying to hit one thousand on weekends when you are off work.
10. Stay comfortable while you write. A comfortable chair, an ergonomic keyboard, sweatpants that are not too tight—these are important. I also love setting myself up with some herbal tea, my water bottle, and healthy snacks. This way, I do not have to get up if I get hungry or thirsty. I set the temperature just right, cover my lap in my favorite blanket, and set my pillow in the small of my back. That way, discomforts do not distract me and pull me away from my writing.
11. Shut out distractions. Turn off your phone, do not answer email alerts that pop up on your desktop, and tell everyone to leave you in peace. Work in a quiet area, or put your headphones on to block out noise. Sometimes, I even use blackout curtains so I do not end up staring off into space out the window. I do not put a lot of distracting things up on my walls in my writing space, either. Distractions break your concentration and tear you away from your writing. They must be avoided at all costs.
12. When you find yourself getting tired or aggravated, take a break. Fifteen minutes should be sufficient to release your stress and approach your writing with fresh eyes again. If you must, you can stop and continue on the next day. Writing should be enjoyable—when it turns ugly, walk away for a while.

No one enjoys sitting and doing the same task for hours on end—that goes for writing, too.
13. Each morning, look at your bigger goals and break them into smaller goals that you can accomplish each day. List them in pencil in the order you wish to complete them and move them around if you must.
14. As you complete tasks, cross them off, and I guarantee you will get a sense of accomplishment. When you feel as if you are making little progress, pause and reflect on these lists. See how much you really have done.

Stop Making Excuses

Okay, I have been there. I have made excuses to put off and get out of writing. I love writing, and I'm not a procrastinator. But there are days I tend to avoid it just like all writers do. I believe it is the mental exertion.

Really, there is no excuse to not write. Have a long flight? Write while you are on the plane. Have shopping to do? Write after shopping. When you find yourself justifying why you are not writing, tell yourself, "I have no excuses!" Then sit down and write, even if it is just a word! One word is better than nothing, and it gets you in gear.

Sometimes you won't feel inspired to write. After a long day, over the holidays or when you have company, you may not want to write. You are too exhausted, distracted, overwhelmed, or whatever else you are feeling. Try and take these experiences and/or emotions and write about them—even if it has nothing to do with your book.

It is okay to take breaks, as long as you have a solid plan and a specific date or time in mind to get back into it. For instance, if you take the holidays off from writing, have a plan to get back to it on a particular date after the holidays are over.

Excuses may be flimsy or valid. But they can derail your progress. Do not give them power.

Wrap-Up

No matter what—write each day. Set aside and make time when you are not busy. Budget time more efficiently now. Writing takes discipline, dedication, and time—be sure to pay attention to all of these things.

Follow my tips, like immersing yourself in writing, creating a peaceful environment free of distractions, and getting comfortable before you write, to foster the discipline you need to adhere to your schedule. Make writing a pleasant experience and you will want to commit to it. There is no need to put writing off or hate it.

Read on to Chapter 7 to learn more about getting motivated, inspired, and ready to write. Learn how to give your *procrastination* something to do! But make sure you finish your action steps for this chapter for your continued success.

Action Steps

1. Determine the best time for you to accomplish productive writing.
2. Set aside time to write each day and stick to it.

3. If you cannot adhere to the time, pick another time for the same day.
4. Create a daily, weekly, monthly, and yearly plan for your writing.
5. Follow the tips above to foster discipline and sanity with your writing journey.

7
MOTIVATION, INSPIRATION, AND PROCRASTINATION

There is no greater agony than bearing an untold story inside of you.
—Maya Angelou

Are you still struggling with finding the time and motivation to write? In Chapter 6, I talked about getting and staying motivated to write by setting aside time, cultivating discipline, and applying yourself.

But there is often more to it than "forcing" yourself to write. You need inspiration for your content, motivation to push through the tough times, and tools to overcome procrastination when it rears its ugly head. This chapter will teach you how to accomplish these three things easily.

Motivation

Since writing a book is a relatively challenging activity, you need motivation to get you through the tough parts. Otherwise, it is far too easy to give up when the going gets tough.

Think back to the whole reason you wanted to write your book.

- You wanted to make a difference for people and their pets
- You wanted to share your compassion for animals with other pet lovers
- You wanted to write a book based on your favorite topic—animals

Now it is time to focus on these three things to gain motivation for writing.

You may have other motives, too. Maybe you want to promote your business, or support your favorite cause. Maybe you want to be able to say, "I'm a writer," or put your English degree to good use. Maybe you promised your blog readers or customers a book, and now you have to write one. Whatever your motives are, they are good ones because they drive you to write.

When you encounter a rough patch with your writing or feel unmotivated to start writing, think about what inspires you. That should get you into an eager frame of mind for writing. But if it fails to get you writing, consider using deadlines and goals as motivation (Chapter 6).

There is no better motivation than having to complete a book by a certain date. When you feel like putting off writing, you can remember you have to finish the book in one, two, or three months. That makes you actually write because you won't finish the book on time otherwise. I often give myself fairly tight deadlines to stay motivated.

Set a writing goal for each day (Chapter 6). Set yourself up to write a certain number of words each day and complete a chapter or section by a set date. This goal will act as motivation. You want to feel a sense of accomplishment when you meet a goal and get to check it off of your list!

Now let's look at ways to inspire you to keep writing when you do not want to write. These ideas will help you if you feel like procrastinating and sabotaging your writing schedule that you created in Chapter 6.

Inspiration

We all have had those really blah days. Days when we do not want to write, cannot think of what to write, and do not feel excited about writing. Certain events and stress can especially rob you of inspiration.

I know after a long day of work or a long trip, I completely lack inspiration. Sometimes, I sign up to write a story for an anthology or collection. I have a deadline, but I just cannot scrounge up the inspiration for a good plot and intriguing characters. When this happens, I sit down and come up with a schedule to keep me inspired.

If you lack inspiration, you are far from alone. Do not feel bad. Here are a few things I do to get my inspiration back—I hope they will work for you.

Step One: Daily Writing Prompts

To write, my mind must be in "writing mode." I am useless if my mind is in "social mode" or "playing with pets mode"—or worse yet, "watching mindless television mode." To get my mind into writing mode, I love to use daily writing prompts.

These prompts are often single sentences or even sentence fragments that compel you to create a story. The prompt may be an opening or closing sentence you must use, or simply an idea to inspire you to get started. Some prompts tell you to write a certain number of words, while others do not have a limit. You can interpret the prompt how you want and create your own unique story.

Examples of Writing Prompts

Here are a few fun writing prompts to get you going with pet fiction or nonfiction. There are hundreds of writing prompts online. Search "writing prompts for animal lovers," or a variation, and you will find a bunch to get you going.

- Write a story about your cat climbing the wall to get a moth
- Write a story about a dog who is a pickpocket
- Write a letter to your avatar (Chapter 2) telling them you are sorry
- Write about your avatar trying out a new activity

Step Two: Writing Challenges

Writing challenges are also incredibly inspiring. There are many you can choose from, and you can find them by doing a Google search. I would suggest finding one that fits your goals, schedule, and genre.

For fiction: "Twelve Short Stories in Twelve Months" is an example of such a challenge (Resources). In this challenge, you must create a story each month of a certain number of words (no more and no less!) centered around a prompt, then post it on the site and receive comments. You must also read and comment on the short stories other people post.

Another popular challenge is "Nanowrimo"(Resources). With this challenge, you must complete a 50,000-word novel in the month of November. There is a Facebook group with people who will support your journey. It can be fun and inspiring.

Finding a challenge can inspire you and get you into writing mode. If you do a Google search for "writing challenges," you will find groups that focus on poetry, fiction, nonfiction, short stories, etc. I listed some of them in the Resources section of this book.

Step 3: Read or Watch a Movie

Reading and watching movies can inspire you to stay focused with your writing as well, as long as you do not use them as methods for procrastination. They are playbooks for how to create plots and characters. Plus, they can inspire you to express your ideas in unique ways.

When I feel stuck, I love to take a break and read for a while. I have several books that I am reading at a time—each one a different genre. No matter what I'm working on in my writing studio, if I feel overwhelmed or stuck, I pick up my Kindle and start reading. Every week, I try to catch a new movie, either on television or in the theater. I urge you to do the same because you never know what you may gain.

Step 4: Take a Writing Course

Writing courses and classes are designed to inspire you. They can be so inspiring you are almost guaranteed confidence, skills, and motivation to create your book for pet lovers and/or professionals. By taking a writing course, you will gain knowledge, camaraderie, and skills.

Some courses are in person, while others are online. Depending on your budget and schedule, find one that you look forward to. Search for a course tailored to your type of writing. For example, a mystery writing course if you are writing a pet cozy mystery. Or a nonfiction research course if you are writing nonfiction.

Look up writing courses online. Also, seek out writing groups on social media, such as Writers Write (Resources). These groups will share details of upcoming courses with you. I included a list of a few online course websites in the Resources section of this book.

Step 5: Experience Something New

New experiences in life are the fodder for books. When you take a trip to Paris, you might get an idea for a lovely romance scene as you walk past quaint coffee shops and view the Eiffel

Tower. When you get together with old friends for a high school reunion, you might hear one of your old classmates share a story about how her life turned out which could spark ideas for how to shape your own character.

Try new things, meet new people, and gain inspiration when you feel stalled on a book. People watching can be an incredible resource for material and inspiration.

In pet writing, new experiences centered around pets can be helpful. Watch a dog obedience class, a team of huskies pull a sled, and/or volunteer at a cat shelter. Try to spend as much time around animals for inspiring ideas. Even trying out new pet-related products can motivate your creative flow.

I have found inspiration tends to come at the strangest times from the most unanticipated sources. Placing yourself in new situations and experiences helps you remain open to inspiration.

Step 6: Take a Break

Sometimes we lose inspiration out of sheer boredom, exhaustion, and repetition. Working on a book for too long can drain you. That is when you need to take a break. Once you do, you can approach your writing with a fresh outlook. When you start to feel bored, exhausted, frustrated, or otherwise negative while writing, put it away and go do something else.

When you take a break, it is important to do things that do not relate to writing or your book at all. You need to exercise, stretch, go for a walk, or partake in a new activity. The key is to get your mind off of your book for a while.

A break may be a few minutes to a few days. I have taken breaks of a few months before. You need to take as long as you need to clear your head. Return when you feel ready.

A break is not admitting defeat. It is not giving up on the book, because you plan to return. But the longer your break is, the harder it can be to get back into "writing mode" and get the motivation and discipline back to sit down and write.

If you take a lengthy break of more than a day, you must set a return date. This date is nonnegotiable. When that date arrives, you must commit to writing once again.

Step 7: Mini Writing Retreats

I love to schedule mini writing retreats for myself. I oftentimes go to the coast of Maine and get an Airbnb for a few days. I turn off all social media, radio, television, etc.

I even schedule stay-at-home writing retreats. This is where I stay at home and cloister myself in my studio. I do not look at social media or do things that distract me. I cook ahead and freeze my food so all I have to do is warm it on the stove.

For both of these writing retreats, I do scheduled breaks, times to talk to my husband if he is not with me, and definitely time for my doggo. Walks on the beach and time spent in nature are incredibly inspiring for me when I am on my retreat.

Step 8: Meet Someone New

New people form the basis for our characters—especially fiction. New people also share stories or do things that can be inspiring. As you get to know new people, or hang out with people you haven't seen in a while, you can gather a lot of details for stories and characters.

When your inspiration runs dry, I highly recommend setting up a social experience of some type. At the very least, go out to a public place and enjoy some people watching.

Step 9: Hire a Writing Coach

Writing coaches have different roles and fulfill different tasks. It is one of my favorite tasks to do for other writers. In my practice, I am geared toward inspiring and motivating people to write and finish their books. I offer inspiration and strategies for overcoming the sense of being stuck. And teach people what you need to know to publish and market.

Some coaches meet in person, and others over the phone or video chat. Fees vary, but a quality writing coach is an investment. Do your research and find one that fits your personality and goals.

You can search for writing coaches online. View their reviews and portfolios to ensure they produce happy and successful writers. If they offer a complimentary session, use this to get to know these coaches better and find one who works well with you.

Step 10: Use Work or Other Mundane Experiences For Inspiration

Your work can be an incredible resource for obscure or mundane material for your book. I am sure there are many other commonplace activities you engage in every day. Ask yourself how you can gain inspiration from:

- Water cooler chitchat about the weather
- Data crunching for hours on end
- Your office mate who sings to himself or herself

A true writer gleans inspiration from everything—even the mundane and banal.

I find relatable stories contain elements from the mundane. Recreating a horribly dull watercooler chat with one of your coworkers can provide priceless comedy to your story, for instance. Look at your daily experiences and see if there is something in them that you can recreate in your story in a meaningful way.

Next is procrastination. This is a real issue that many writers face. It can be easy to let procrastination take hold of your writing journey and sabotage you from moving forward. Read on to learn ways to beat procrastination.

Beat Procrastination

Procrastination is hardly a rare experience. It is an annoying and limiting habit that many of us fall victim to. When you do not want to write, you tend to put it off, and the next thing you know, years have passed.

Overcoming procrastination can feel like beating the laws of gravity, but here are some tips I use when I want to put off my writing tasks for the day.

Step One: Write—Right Now

When you catch yourself putting writing off or dreading it, do not wait any longer—it just lets the inertia build. No matter where you are, open up your computer or notebook and get to work. Instead of letting yourself put writing off, do it the minute you want to procrastinate and replace inaction with action.

Even if you have already missed your daily writing time, as discussed in the previous chapter, it is never too late to write. At least get a few words done before you turn in for the night. Doing something is better than nothing! As soon as you think about writing—get to work.

Step Two: Set Clear Goals With Due Dates

It is harder to put off a clear goal than a vague one. Consider the difference between these two goals:

I want to write something today.

I want to write five hundred words by 2:00 p.m.

Which one is more motivating? Which one actually makes it clear what you must do and when? The latter goal is more likely to make you think, "Okay, all I have to do is five hundred words. I have two hours left to do it. I better get to it now!"

Each day, set a goal for your writing. Set a number, the topic, and a time. Look at your book outline and set similar goals for each part of the book. When you do this, you can overcome procrastination and complete the book by your deadline.

Step Three: Track Progress

As you complete goals, be sure to check them off in a planner or to-do list or on your calendar. This gives you a sense of accomplishment and lets you see your progress. Seeing progress is inspiring and creates momentum because you think, "I already did this much, and it was not so bad!"

With each item checked off your to-do list, you will feel eager to check off more items until you are finished. You see it is possible and painless—then you want to get your writing done. Tracking your progress makes it harder to see the value in putting writing off.

Step Four: Create a Reward

One thing I like to do is tell myself, "I can go for an extra-long hike with my dog, Addie, only *after* I meet my writing goal today." That way, I have something to look forward to after I write. It makes me want to complete my writing faster so I can play with my best friend.

When you want to put off writing because you think you may have something better to do, make your better thing wait until you finish writing. Make writing a priority, and reserve your other activity for a reward. This tricks your brain into completing the goal.

Step Five: Journal or Write Some Other Way

When you make your life about writing, it gets easier to find the motivation to write. Even if you are not working on your book at the moment, make yourself write a blog article, submit stories to competitions, and journals.

Also, you can read writing articles and watch videos. Attend courses and meet with other writers. Post in social media writing groups and read the posts other people make. All of these things keep you writing, and you can find it easier to overcome procrastination.

Wrap-Up

We covered a lot in this chapter, and you can refer to it often as you need help. There will probably be something new to inspire you each time you feel unmotivated.

Although, it can be hard to find motivation to write—keep in mind your motivation lies in your purpose with your pet book. Being clear with your purpose keeps your motivation alive and helps you to move forward.

There are many places you can find inspiration. Inspiration is easy to come by—even in the mundane. Be open to all possibilities. You can use your life experiences to create awesome scenes in your fiction or tips to help people with obscure issues in nonfiction.

Please, when you feel like procrastinating, do not do it. Set clear goals and intentions for writing, track your progress, journal, and do whatever it takes to overcome procrastination.

In the next chapter, learn about writing your rough draft. Remember, your rough draft is supposed to be rough! You are not ready for publication yet, so have fun with it and get your ideas down. Your final book will look better when you completely finish.

Here are your action steps to cultivate motivation, inspiration, and nab procrastination.

Action Steps

1. Discover your motivation. Why do you want to write your book?
2. Write your motivation down and pin it to the wall of your writing studio where you can see it.
3. Figure out what will block or stall your writing process and determine a solution for each. Focus on those positive solutions.
4. Get inspired when you feel dull—through new experiences, new friends, books, movies, writing coaches, and writing prompts or challenges.
5. Do not let procrastination win—ever. Set goals, track progress, and make time for writing in your life.

8

YOUR ROUGH DRAFT

The rough draft of anything is garbage.
—*Ernest Hemingway*

Are you tempted to edit your rough draft, trying to make it perfect along the way? Please stop attempting to make your first draft a polished masterpiece. Honestly, it will drive you crazy, and you may never get your ideas on paper—or worse yet, your manuscript done.

I am going to help you write your rough draft with the tools I use myself and what I share with my clients. Your first goal after creating your outline is writing a rough draft—not a polished piece. But I promise I will help you with creating such a manuscript in Chapter 9.

A Rough Draft

A rough draft is the first draft of your book—the messy skeleton of what your book will become. It will not look great, but it is positively brimming with potential. I cannot tell you how many drafts you will write—it depends on you as the writer and your topic.

Some books may be done after one draft, while others take up to twenty. Personally, I go through my nonfiction drafts about five times and my fiction ten times. Since this draft is your creation, it will grow, evolve, and change.

Hence, there is absolutely no pressure to write a perfect, beautiful rough draft. It is called "rough" for a reason. I like to write mine quickly and sloppily—then improve upon it later.

Write to Get it Done

The purpose of the rough draft is to get your ideas down on paper quickly. You want to get your ideas down, create some substance for the book, and give yourself something to work on and improve later.

Writing your rough draft is where you use all the tools you learned in Section I:

- Figuring out the subject or themes of your writing
- Fiction or nonfiction
- Creating your avatar
- Mind mapping techniques
- Outlining
- Developing character profiles for fiction

This draft does not need to be perfect, heartfelt, or ready for publication. But you do need to get your ideas, wisdom, and/or story written down to get your book started. Keep in mind, the polishing of your work will come later.

Using your outline, start to expand on the ideas you have already written (Chapter 4). Start each chapter with Dear, your avatar's name (Chapter 2). Using your outline, *talk* to your avatar briefly or in full detail—it does not matter. As long as you create the bulk of your content and get your ideas down on paper.

It is important to write and let the ideas flow. Do not pause to self-edit, as that can stop your forward motion and throttle the flow of ideas. Instead, ignore the mistakes and move on. I have been known to write sentence fragments to capture a main idea and move on. This is not the time to craft lovely sentences.

Of course, if you come up with a beautiful passage or lovely sentence—write it! You will forget it if you wait—trust me. As ideas occur to you, you must capture them. You want all of your ideas on paper so you do not forget them.

The length of your rough draft may not match the length you want your book to be. It may be too long or too short. That is okay. You can identify the disparity in the next draft and either add or take away content as needed.

Longhand

If you want to get your ideas onto paper without electronics—try longhand for your rough draft. Your handwriting does not need to be beautiful, as long as you can read it. Later, you can type and refine it. The point of the rough draft is getting everything down—longhand allows you to accomplish this goal.

Some people work better with longhand. Later, they hire someone to type their work, or they type it themselves. Authors have told me they feel a stronger connection between their brain and writing as long as they are writing by hand. If you are such a person, then go for it!

My greatest fear as a writer is losing my work if I did my rough drafts in longhand. Once you write stuff down, you never know what could happen to your pages. Scan them or take pictures as a form of backup. Store finished pages in a safe drawer, as well.

Computer

Typing your rough draft is the easiest way, in my opinion. If you are not great at typing, you probably will be by the end of your book! What is nice about writing your rough draft on a computer is you have many tools at your fingertips to make the process quicker and easier.

You can use spell check and punctuation to make corrections, you are able to back up your work in different locations immediately, and you can also print your work if you feel more comfortable self-editing on paper—which many of my clients do.

If you want to be able to access your draft anywhere, consider using Google Docs or any cloud-based word processor. As long as you have Internet, you can work on your document. Plus, you can easily share the document with your team, such as editors, proofreaders, and beta readers. If you use Word (which I prefer), set it up to sync with your OneDrive or some other cloud storage. Your work is saved even if your computer crashes.

However, these documents can be hard to retrieve if you are offline. Be sure to enable offline functionality or else copy and paste your cloud document into Word to access when you are not online.

Always save often and back up your writing! There is nothing worse than working hard on a draft, then suffering a hard drive crash and losing it. Never make the mistake of saving everything in one place or this could happen to you. Imagine the setback. It may be enough to make you give up on your pet book.

Fortunately, with today's cloud storage technology, it is easy to save your work in multiple locations for retrieval anywhere, anytime, on any device. I recommend saving a copy of your draft in several databases—Google Docs, OneDrive, and Dropbox, for example.

Recording Your Words

Another fantastic option for writing your rough draft is to record yourself. This option is great if you are finding it difficult to sit down and write (Chapter 6). My clients love this alternative if they commute to work.

Oftentimes, my clients who record their rough draft finish their manuscripts quicker than they anticipated, and their books are finished ahead of schedule.

After you are done dictating your draft, you can transcribe the recordings or have someone transcribe them for you. Recording lets you get your ideas documented quickly when you are pressed for writing time.

I love recording my rough draft when I'm walking my dog. This way, none of my ideas are lost, and I do not have to carry a notebook. It is also convenient when I'm on the go and get an idea.

You cannot always write—but you can quickly record your ideas. Use your phone's recording app, a camcorder, or other recording device you have at hand. Store the recordings with clear labels about their content so you can find them later. There is nothing more annoying than sifting through tons of unlabeled audio files—trust me.

I recommend backing up your recordings in a cloud. That way you never lose anything important. You can also access your recordings anywhere and anytime you may need them.

When you are ready to turn your spoken words into written ones, you can hire a transcriptionist on a site like Upwork or Fiverr (Resources). Otherwise, you can transcribe them yourself.

Please remember, do not worry about self-editing until you get everything down. This is still a rough draft!

A Letter to Your Avatar

I discussed writing a "Dear Avatar" letter to craft each of your chapters during the rough draft phase in Chapter 2. This can make your writing journey seamless once you get the hang of this tool.

Of course, you wouldn't keep the same format in your final draft, but this is a writing prompt (Chapter 7) that is priceless and a surefire way to keep you on track with your writing.

Wrap-Up

Your rough draft is your chance to get your ideas down and start writing your manuscript. It is important during this step to not self-edit or try to make things perfect. Your goal is to get your rough draft done.

You will be able to go back once completed and polish your thoughts and words. Keep in mind, shorthand notes and sentence fragments are acceptable. As long as you get your ideas down, you are accomplishing the purpose of your draft.

You can work longhand, on a computer, or by recording yourself. Find the way you are comfortable with. While I generally use a computer for my writing, I am known to jot down longhand notes or record myself in a pinch when my laptop is not readily at hand. You can thus combine methods to ensure you never forget a great idea.

After you complete the action steps for this chapter, get ready for self-editing. I love the self-editing process. I find inspiration while in this phase of creativity. Next, you will learn all my steps to getting my manuscript polished and ready for my editor.

Action Steps

1. Take a look at the schedule you created in Chapter 6 and start writing without editing anything.
2. Pick whether you want to write longhand, use a computer, or record yourself to complete your rough draft.
3. Consider a combination of methods to fit your schedule and lifestyle.
4. Start each chapter as a Dear Avatar letter.
5. Always make copies of your notes, recordings, or typed documents. Save often and in many locations, online and offline.
6. Remember, the purpose of your rough draft is to get your ideas on paper by using the tools I helped you with in Section I. It is not a manuscript ready for an editor. You will learn how to prepare your manuscript for an editor in the next chapter.

9

CLEAN UP YOUR ROUGH DRAFT

Writing without revising is the literary equivalent of waltzing gaily out of the house in your underwear.
—Patricia Fuller

Did you know you have to prepare your manuscript and perform some basic, yet rigorous self-editing before you send in your book for editing? Professional editors expect your book to be in a certain state of readability—you cannot send them your raw rough drafts.

I have a lot of respect for good editors, but I must say—editors can be tough. And we want them to be. They are not inclined to tolerate little annoyances they clearly ask you not to do in their submission guidelines.

In my experience, editors do not like staples (for a printed manuscript), small print, and terrible grammar—among many other things. To foster a good relationship with your editor, you want to get familiar with how to polish your manuscript for submission. The good news is—the more you self-edit your manuscript, the better the editing job.

Your editor will be able to perform his or her job more thoroughly if your book is already prepared. It is quite difficult for someone to slog through pages of poorly prepared and error-ridden writing. Your book does not have to be perfect—perfecting it is the editor's job—but it needs to be readable and presentable.

This chapter is about how to turn your rough draft into a final manuscript for the editor. Again, I cannot tell you how many drafts you will go through, but you will know when you have completed your manuscript. Once you feel confident your work imparts your message and is self-edited, you can move on to sending it to an editor.

Let's go over the basic steps to prepare your manuscript for editing.

Self-Editing

With your rough draft completed, you will start at the beginning and self-edit for the first time. This is where you fill out missing information or passages, add reference notes if applicable, and correct glaring errors. You might move sentences or whole paragraphs around and reorganize the book.

Steps For Self-Editing

Step One: I change the font to something easy to read, like Courier or Arial. I highlight the entire manuscript and then set the font size to twelve. Next, I go to "Paragraph" and set the line spacing to double.

I save this. Now my manuscript is much easier to self-edit. I am able to spot errors that are harder to see with fonts like Times New Roman and Georgia. However, these are my personal preferences. You can play around with fonts and sizes to find the one that is easiest for you.

Step Two: Go through your manuscript from the beginning. I like to break it up into sections and do a section each day. It removes the stress from what otherwise seems like an overwhelming task. You will find what works for you. I also recommend you keep a notebook by your side to take notes, as you will probably come up with many. I like to note things that I notice or need to check on later in the document.

When you complete this part, you will be able to take a break. I recommend a break because self-editing can be vexing and time-consuming. You want to tackle it for the second round with a fresh pair of eyes. Put it down and come back when you feel refreshed and renewed. I cannot tell you specifically how long this may take, but you will know.

Step Three: You will repeat this self-editing process a second time. This time, you will be looking for errors you overlooked the first time. This is the point in self-editing where I read my manuscript aloud for the first time. Keep in mind, initially you still have to read to yourself to clean up your manuscript.

When you read aloud, you will be surprised with how much more you can pick up. Reading aloud is a tool you do not want to skip prior to sending your manuscript to your editor.

Plus, as you read through a second time, you become even

more familiar with the manuscript and how to better present the information or story. You will be able to make more adjustments to have it flow soundly. Take another break, and then return for the third round of self-editing.

Step Four: The third time is the charm—usually. The third time lets you catch those little errors you tend to overlook because you knew what you meant to say.

At this point, I also like to run the book through ProWritingAid (Resources) to find any errors I still have not caught. A proofreading software is not as perfect or accurate as your own eyes or an editor. However, it can catch little things like common misspellings, misused words, run-on sentences, and passive grammar. It is an additional layer of self-editing to help you smooth out your writing.

Step Five: Watch for topic changes by reading your manuscript aloud—again! What looks good on paper does not always sound as good aloud. You need to read your book aloud at least two times in the self-editing process to make sure it flows. (I read mine three to five times.) By flow, I mean the manuscript reads cohesively, and one point leads into the next nicely.

As you read, watch out for sudden topic changes (nonfiction) or plot holes (fiction). If your work does not make sense, you are either tired, you switch topics too quickly, or you neglected to clear up something in the plot, thus creating a plot hole (Glossary). If this is apparent to you, your reader will have the same experience.

Consider adding some sort of transition sentence or paragraph signaling to the reader you are changing topics. Read it over again and notice how much more smoothly the book reads.

Step Six: Also, watch out for clunky sentences as you continue polishing your manuscript. If you lose your breath by the end of a sentence, it is too long and will lose a reader's attention. Meanwhile, if your sentences sound choppy and staccato, they are too short.

A blend of short and longer sentences provides the best cadence for the book. Some of your sentences may be worded awkwardly and need to be fixed. Read clunky sentences aloud, and if they do not feel right, then try rephrasing the sentence different ways while speaking aloud until you find the best word order.

Step Seven: Watch out for confusing pronouns. If you read "he" and have to go back to figure out who you are referring to, it is time to replace "he" with the subject's actual name. Avoid starting too many sentences with "It" for the same reason.

Step Eight: A big one to watch out for is a tautology (Glossary). This is where you say something twice in different ways. For example, "my own horse" is a tautology. All you have to say is "my horse." Adding "own" is repetitive and simply reiterates the fact that this is your horse.

You can eliminate a lot of wordiness and annoyingly long sentences by cutting out tautologies. Furthermore, you can find wordy phrases and replace them with more succinct, action-packed ones. Such as replacing "I decided to act" with "I acted." These two things exponentially improve flow.

Step Nine: Beware of passive or vague grammar. For your

writing to engage readers, it must have action that is clearly assigned to a character or subject within the book.

As you read aloud, notice if you have any sentences that sound like:

"Many dogs are not taken care of, so they get sick and do not act right."

This sentence is pretty vague—who is not taking care of these dogs, and what precisely happens as a result?

Replace with:

"You may not know how to take care of your dog, which leads to many behavioral problems and health issues."

See what difference an action verb makes? The passive is sleepy and unclear—action makes your reader feel engaged.

Step Ten: Finally, try to catch when you repeat the same word too many times. A thesaurus, either online or in book form, is handy here. If you keep catching yourself reading the same word over and over, you will feel bored, and your reader will be bored as well.

Consider replacing some of the words with synonyms or appropriate pronouns. As I said before, do not start every sentence the same with "It" or "This," as that is repetitive and boring. Spicier language is always more entertaining and engaging for readers.

Ready For Beta Readers?

If you want—when your book is smooth enough where you do not feel embarrassed to show it to other people—call on a few good beta readers. Personally, I wait until I get it back from the professional proofreader (Chapter 10).

If this is your first book—I would suggest asking a good friend, family member, or fellow writer to read and comment before you send it to your editor. Make it clear they only need to read it without editing. Their job is to ensure the book makes sense and to point out any extremely obvious flaws or issues. They are not supposed to nitpick the font or argue with you about the Oxford comma.

I suggest to my clients to offer their manuscripts to beta readers at this point in Arial with double spaces and no indents. Your preliminary beta readers can jot notes in the columns or over sentences as they read (hard copy). However, they can make comments in the margins when you put the manuscript in Google Docs or send as a Word doc.

A literary group is a great place to find beta readers and fellow writers who are eager to read and give useful tips. You can find them online or meet with them in person. The group should build you up and help you improve—not intimidate you or insult you. However, I suggest only reaching out to this type of audience when you have a final manuscript that is ready for publication or when you already have published a few books.

Prepare Your Manuscript For Your Editor

When you write your manuscript, you can use whatever font and formatting you wish to make the book easy to work on. As you self-edit, you want to use the specifications I stated above. But when you are about to send it off for editing, you must undo any special formatting and prepare the book in a simple style that the editor can easily use.

All editors and proofreaders have their own specific formatting requirements. You can easily find these out and then make the required changes to your book. But if your editor does not specify any particular format, here is a basic one that most editors will accept.

1. Set the color to black and the font to Arial. You do not need fancy colors or fonts right now. Those are distracting to an editor, who is more concerned with the actual content. You can add that later on in the design part.
2. Set your page size to 8.5 x 11 and set your margins to one inch on all sides. This is standard in the industry. Again, you can change all of that in the design stage.
3. Align it to left justified. This makes the left side uniform and the right nonuniform.
4. Remove double spaces after periods. Some people still type like this because that is how things were done in the days of typewriters. But now in the computer age, double spacing is unnecessary. You can easily remove this by simply going to "Find and Replace," entering a period and two spaces in the find bar, and then entering a period and a single space in the replace bar. Hit enter, and the document will become formatted accordingly. Be sure to scroll through a few pages to make sure your changes stuck. Also, be sure to save after each formatting change!
5. Get rid of tabs. Again you can use "Find and Replace" for this. Replace tabs with five spaces on the

space bar. Be sure to indent all new paragraphs if your book is fiction. Otherwise, do not indent paragraphs at all. Use a single space between paragraphs to separate them instead.

6. Bold and left justify all headings. Be sure to enter a page break between each new chapter, instead of hitting the return key dozens of times to create a new page. The page break will keep the spaces in any format, while hitting the return key will not.

7. Add page numbers. Select the option for a number on the top left of your page. Start numbering on the page your story or book starts, not on the title page. Add a table of contents at the beginning of the book with page numbers when you have finished numbering. To auto-generate one in Google Docs, you want to make each chapter heading "Heading 1" and each subheading "Heading 2." Subheadings under these can be "Heading 3."

Pages to Include

Your manuscript is not complete without the addition of pages called front matter and back matter (Glossary). Basically, front matter are the pages in your manuscript before the main text of your nonfiction or fiction book. Back matter are the pages at the end of your book.

Here are some suggestions of what to include—not everything is necessary. I suggest you do your own research as well. Look at some of the books you love for what the author includes in their front and back pages. Those marked with * are necessary.

Front Matter

- Title Page*
- Copyright Page*
- Table of Contents*
- Forward/Preface
- Introduction*

Back Matter

- Conclusion*
- Glossary
- Resources
- Acknowledgements*
- About the Author*
- Review Request Page*
- More Books by Author*

You are now ready to send the whole document in one file. Do not send separate files for each chapter. If you print your work, do not staple them, as that is the bane of any editor's existence.

Follow Submission Guidelines

In Chapter 10, I will go into how to find a great editor and proofreader. But for now, know this—each editor has his or her own guidelines and rules for submissions. You would be wise to follow these rules. Some editors are flexible—others not. You will find some want a printed, double-spaced manuscript delivered by mail and others want electronic submissions of .docx or Google Docs files.

The important thing is finding out what your editor really wants. He or she will usually post it clearly on his or her website and/or in your contract. Otherwise, you can ask the editor directly. Follow the instructions, and make the editorial process a smooth one by staying on your editor's good side.

Wrap-Up

To get your book ready for publication—self-edit your manuscript thoroughly. Do not skimp on this process. The more you polish your manuscript, the easier it will be for your editor to suggest changes.

I provided you with steps and suggestions in this chapter. It is important to present your editor with a polished and a self-edited manuscript. You will get a better product in return, and it may even cost you less.

If this is your first book, finding a beta reader at this point is a good idea. But if you are a seasoned self-published author, I would wait until you have your *ready to publish* manuscript.

If you want, you can ask family and friends who love animals to provide objective criticism and make sure the book makes sense. But honestly, I would not depend on them to do this for you. Instead, you might want to hire someone from Fiverr or Upwork to get the job done quicker (Resources).

After you do the action steps for this chapter, go to Section III: What's Next for Success. I will start this section by explaining different types of editors, then go on to how to design the interior of your book, create a winning cover, upload to Amazon, and market your book.

Action Steps

1. Prepare your manuscript for self-editing by picking a font and size that works for you.
2. Go through your rough draft at least three to five times—rework sentences, flow (nonfiction), plot (fiction), grammar, organization, etc.
3. Read your work out loud at least twice and make more self-edits.
4. If you are a first-time writer, consider having a few friends or family members read your manuscript—ask them to comment on the flow only.
5. Prepare your manuscript to meet submission guidelines of your specific editor.

SECTION III

WHAT'S NEXT FOR SUCCESS

Are you inspired to go to the next step? Are you excited to be so close to self-publishing your book?

With your manuscript self-edited and ready for the editor, you can finally let out a long sigh of relief and take a break. All your hard work deserves a celebration. You definitely need to pat yourself on the back. But, as you know, this is not the end—yet.

In this section, I am going to guide you with ways to transform your book from a professionally edited manuscript to an actual self-published book for pet lovers and/or professionals. Whether you are writing an ebook or a print book, you still need to take steps to get it edited, proofread, formatted, and published.

If you do not know the first thing about self-publishing, do not worry. I did not know anything when I wrote my first book. But now I am a self-published author with over twelve best-selling books (and counting) in multiple genres. Plus, I help other writers reach their dreams of becoming a published author.

I will teach you how to find your editor, formatter, and cover designer. You will learn how to launch and market your book to pet lovers and pet professionals. From designing your cover to marketing—I will cover it. Read on to learn how to get your book for pet lovers and/or pet professionals self-published.

It is now time to take your manuscript to the next level—publication!

10

FIND YOUR EDITORS

Everyone needs an editor.
—*Tim Foote*

Are you overwhelmed with trying to find your team of editors? As the author, you are the brains behind your book. You definitely served an important role. But your book won't come to existence without the careful work of other professionals on your side. You must assemble a team to create an outstanding pet book that sells well—including editors.

Your team is going to consist of many different people who offer different services. It all starts with your team of editors and ends with your launch team (Chapter 13).

In this chapter, I present different types of editors available to get your manuscript finalized for publication. You may not need to hire all of them, but keep in mind each one is instrumental in your book's final success. Be sure to find great people, whether you are writing fiction or nonfiction.

Developmental Editor

A developmental editor has a specific job. His or her main task is editing your book for structure or plot. They will look at big-picture elements such as consistency, flow, structure, readability, and clarity for your fiction or nonfiction book. Basically, they make sure your manuscript is structured properly.

Primarily, this type of editor will provide pointers and feedback on what sections or paragraphs should be deleted, revised, or moved so that your point is clear or your plot is solid.

He or she will also point out things like, "This dialogue is stilted. Perhaps try this," or "Your point is not clear here. Let's try this instead to present your point."

A developmental editor may simply help you with your final draft, or he or she may be present for the entire book from rough draft to finished draft. You need to decide when you need help and reach out to a developmental editor at the appropriate time.

Do not wait too long to get help—there is nothing wrong with seeking a professional to help make your book amazing. Especially if you are new to writing, hiring a developmental editor can make your writing process infinitely easier.

Content Editor

A content editor is one in which you hire after you made all the changes your developmental editor has made. This type of editor will make the necessary corrections concerning the flow and paragraph-level content of your presented manuscript. Content editing does not restructure your story or chapters. Rather, they address issues of clarity and consistency within the content of your manuscript.

A content editor will go through your manuscript and correct:

- Clarity
- Syntax
- Voice
- Tense
- Flow

Once a content editor goes through you work and you receive it back from them, I can guarantee you will need to reword sentences and paragraphs to improve your final product.

Copy Or Line Editor

After the structure and content are addressed, it's time to move on to the sentence-level edits. This is where a copy or line editor comes in.

They will:

- Improve phrasing and resolve incorrect word usage
- Resolve inconsistent and inaccurate punctuation
- Improve sentence flow and clarity
- Look for spelling and grammatical errors

What I love about a copy or line editor is they are laser focused. They have an exceptional talent for going through your manuscript line by line to be sure your words look polished and professional.

Proofreader

Finally, proofreaders. This is the stage of editing where the final set of eyes scans your manuscript for errors. They are a lifesaver in bringing your book together and making it ready for publication.

Their main job is to look for errors involving:

- Spelling
- Grammar
- Typos
- Consistency
- Punctuation

Be sure to choose a proofreader that has been formally trained and certified by a body such as the Editorial Freelancers Association or the International Association of Professional Book Editors (Resources). These associations require members to pass rigorous tests and pay fees in order to join.

Anyone can read a book and fix the glaring errors, but a true proofreader will examine your book closely in an effort to catch every little mistake. They will analyze every word and every sentence to ensure correctness.

It is best to contact a proofreading association, like the ones above, to find a vetted member. The proofreader will be able to provide you a portfolio and reviews of past work. He or she should have a professional website that makes his or her process and terms clear.

Wrap-Up

Be sure to manage your expectations for each type of editor you hire. The goal of all editors is to make your book better—but you cannot expect your proofreader to do developmental editing. A proofreader is strictly for improving the spelling, grammar, and punctuation.

To have a record of what was communicated between you and your editor I suggest using email as the primary form of communication rather than telephone or video chat. I consider it a preferred method as do my editors.

Your editor may also be open to using something like Google Docs that makes it easy to see your editor's suggestions and to share comments. You can also access it anywhere. Keep in mind, though, changing the document while the editor is working on it will only slow them down and may even decrease their accuracy.

You can find developmental editors as well as the others mentioned in the chapter on Upwork, Guru, or Fiverr (Resources). You can also look them up online and peruse their websites. A professional website that lists their credentials and best-selling books are good signs that someone is a qualified practitioner. Be sure to take testimonials into account.

Your editor must also be open to a confidentiality agreement such as an NDA, or non-disclosure agreement. This agreement states he or she will not share or reproduce your work without your written permission, not even as a sample in his or her portfolio.

He or she must be transparent about rates and what services you will receive within a specified time frame. Do not expect editors to be cheap—for quality work, be prepared to spend money for good editors.

As you can see, editors are instrumental in preparing your manuscript for publication. If you are unsure what type of editing you need, reach out to an editor and ask. Before you go on to the next step and learn how to design your book, take a look at your action steps for this chapter.

Action Steps

1. Whether you are writing a fiction or nonfiction book for pet lovers and/or professionals, research various types of editors you may need.
2. Ask other writers for references.
3. Be clear with your expectations for what you need for editing. Example: Do not expect a copy editor to do developmental editing.
4. Research various editors online and review their policies, approach, and pricing.
5. Be sure you hire professionally trained editors for your manuscript.
6. Ask for a sample of an editor's work. Expect to pay for a short sample.
7. Know exactly what your editor's expectations are of you.

8. Be sure you have a contract with your editor that outlines pricing, deadlines, communication frequency, etc.
9. Refer back to Chapter 9 to be sure you provide your first editor with a self-edited manuscript.

11

DESIGN YOUR BOOK

Good design is good business.
—*Thomas Watson, Jr.*

Congratulations, you now have a well-edited and polished manuscript—are you ready for the next step? You are now ready to hire a formatter and the cover designer for your book.

Writing a best-selling book for animal lovers and/or professionals is not a job you can accomplish on your own. To make your book ready for self-publishing, you must hire a good team of professionals. We covered editors in Chapter 10. Now I am going to help you with hiring your formatter and cover designer.

You can attempt these things on your own, but the results will always be better with dedicated professionals who know what they are doing—especially the first time around. Be sure to shop around to find professionals who meet your needs and communicate clearly throughout the working relationship.

Book Formatter

A book formatter is a professional or a software app like Vellum (Resources). This person or app designs the interior of your professionally edited manuscript. They set the font, the headings, spacing, etc. Basically, they create an interior layout that is inviting to your reader.

Kindle and print books are formatted differently for Amazon. When you format a manuscript for Kindle or softcover, you need to know what you are doing because inconsistencies can occur. For instance:

- Spaces can become altered
- Images can become aligned weirdly
- Chapter headings may not sit where you want them
- And more

Furthermore, you will have a massive headache when Amazon rejects your images for not having the right DPI. Or when it insists a single sentence on page fifty-nine does not match margin specifications—even though you cannot see the issue on your end.

Since formatting for the first time has a huge learning curve, it is easy to become discouraged. I would wait until you have written a few books before you take this task on.

The easier way to make your book look beautiful is by hiring a professional formatter. They have the patience and expertise to deal with Word's and Amazon's idiosyncrasies. They know exactly how to lay the book out and format it across all mediums.

The formatter will size and lay out images, fancy texts, text bars, blurbs, and more. Their expertise will allow you to upload your manuscript to a self-publishing platform with no problem. You should not encounter issues with spacing, font size, font style, or images after a formatter works on your book.

If your book does not contain images, then you may be able to read up on Amazon's specifications and format your book accordingly by yourself. But when it comes to images, I do not waste any time. I leave it to the pros. Formatting requires a special set of skills that can be elusive, and even infuriating, to the rest of us.

To hire a formatter, ask your editor and author friends for recommendations. Also visit the Internet and search for book formatters. There are many formatting companies to choose from—get recommendations.

Formatters should have portfolios that display samples taken from books they have formatted. They may also be willing to format one page of your book for free to show off their skills. Look for professional, sleek formatting and great testimonials when making your decision on who to hire. Also consider rates; cheap formatters are seldom worth the money you save because you will end up having to hire another one—I've been there!

You may need to meet with your formatter in person or over a video conference to discuss your expectations. But the work can be done entirely over the Internet. A good formatter will go through your book, choose a few different formats that may suit it, and then let you decide which one you like best.

Before hiring a formatter, ask these questions:

1. What is your fee and payment structure?
2. What services do you provide for this fee?
3. What is your turnaround time?
4. What is your formatting process?
5. Can you format the book for both Kindle and print?
6. Will you be able to provide more than one format?
7. How will you deliver the formatted book?
8. What is your process for revisions? Do you charge for revisions?
9. Do you have a no-risk money-back guarantee if I am not satisfied with the work?
10. Can you provide samples and references?
11. Have you formatted a book in my genre before?
12. Can you format one page of my book as a sample?

When you enter a contract with a formatter, be sure to have an NDA, or non-disclosure agreement, in place. Since the formatter has access to your book in its entirety, you have to protect your rights to the content.

Professional formatters should already have NDAs in place that establish all of these terms, and you can go through the NDA and determine what you agree or disagree with. An NDA is a legal contract, and you can use it in court if any part of it is violated, so take it seriously and never work without one.

Additionally, be sure the formatter will provide all agreed-upon services for the agreed-upon fee by a certain date. Make it clear that you will retain all rights to the book and whether or not you will credit the formatter.

Finally, make it clear if the formatter may use any part of your book for a portfolio sample to show other prospective clients or not.

Cover Designer

When your first book is fully written, edited, and formatted into its full potential, you can begin the cover design stage. If you are already a pro at self-publishing, you can do this during the editing period or even before you write your book.

This is such a fun part of the book publishing process—again, one of my favorites! This is where you give your book its unique aesthetic appeal—a cover that makes your book stand out from the other pet books.

They say to never judge a book by its cover, but we all know the cover helps sell a book. Professional cover designers are experts at creating covers that sell your book. A boring, bland cover or a cover that is irrelevant to the book's contents will not entice anyone to buy it.

You want to create a cover that tells people:

- What to expect
- What your book will offer them
- What problem your book can solve

A good idea is to create a cover featuring the type of animal your book is about. A fiction cover might be artistic, while a nonfiction cover might be realistic. Come up with a concept to share with your cover designer. If you have no clue what to do for your cover, many cover designers can propose some ideas and let you pick what you like best.

Cover designers are graphic artists with massive amounts of talent. Like all artists, different designers will have different styles and skills. You want to find the one who can deliver the cover that matches your vision the best. Shop through the portfolios of cover designers and see if any of them can deliver what you want.

Do not jump into a working relationship with the first cover designer someone refers you to. Shop around. First, get referrals from authors you know, your editors, and other people in the publishing industry. Check out the designers' websites and portfolios.

You can also use a site like Fiverr (Resources) to find a cover designer seeking a gig. There are also job bid sites like Guru, Upwork, and 99designs (Resources). They host many designers from all over the world eager for work. Mark's List or Smashwords (Resources) is another source of cover designers, formatters, and others up for hire.

Finally, a simple Internet search can yield some designers with websites where you can view portfolios, rates, and reviews. When you have found a few who match the style you like, approach them for a quote. This is an interview process, so you want to ask some questions:

1. Can I see your complete portfolio?
2. Do you have any references I can speak to?
3. Have you designed covers for my genre before?

4. How will you come up with the concept for my design?
5. How will you create the design?
6. What is your fee range?
7. What is your design process like?
8. Do you do the artwork yourself or have access to a stock photo site?
9. Will you be able to create custom images that I will have full rights to?
10. Do you offer a no-risk money-back guarantee if I am not happy with the work?
11. How will you deliver the final product?
12. What is your turnaround time?
13. Are you available for additional projects if I need them? (This can come in handy in forming long-term relationships with a great designer who can design covers for all of your books, either in a series or not.)
14. Will you give me more than a few covers so that I can change covers to boost sales at any point?

If you like the designer's work and process, can afford the fees, and see primarily great testimonials, then you should initiate the contract. Each designer is different with how he or she likes to handle contracts.

Your contract should outline expectations, types of files, payment schedule, copyright to images, deadlines, etc.

Clear communication is also essential. Cover designers may be experts in the field of cover design, but they are not mind readers. You cannot expect them to know what you want unless you state it clearly. If you do not like a cover concept that someone submits to you, be sure to tell him or her why so that he or she can fix the issue and meet your expectations.

You not only need to communicate your vision for the cover, but you also need to communicate the format and size of your book. Designers can create different sizes and covers that are formatted for ebooks and softcovers. You have to specify what you need.

It is perfectly possible to do this part yourself. But you must become familiar with how to use a design software and size the cover image to fit your book properly. I always leave this part for the pros—I don't want to risk having an unprofessional-looking cover.

Wrap-Up

Writing a best-selling book for pet lovers and/or pet professionals is not a job you can accomplish on your own. To make your book ready for self-publishing, you must hire a good team of professionals—including formatters and cover designers.

You can attempt these things on your own, but the results will always be better with dedicated professionals who know what they are doing—especially your first time with self-publishing. Be sure to shop around to find professionals who meet your needs, communicate clearly throughout the working relationship, and establish an NDA and clear contract before you start working together.

Read on to learn how to create a website to help market your book and boost sales. In this modern age of Internet, you must have a web presence to make it as a pet writer—or any type of writer. But check out your action steps below to be assured you hire the best formatter and cover designer for your masterpiece first.

Action Steps

1. Research formatters and cover designers by asking your editors, fellow authors, and using the Internet for referrals.
2. When hiring your formatter and cover designer, be sure to acquire an NDA and contract.
3. Ask your potential formatter and cover designer for samples of their work.
4. Ask them for testimonials from other clients.
5. Be clear about your needs, expectations, and deliverables at the beginning of the hiring process.
6. If you have published books before, consider using an app called Vellum (Resources), which is especially great for fiction. If you know what you are doing, it works with nonfiction as well.

12

CREATE A WEBSITE AND LANDING PAGE

Do not think of your website as a self-promotion machine, think of it as a self-invention machine.
—Austin Kleon

Have you created your website yet? If you are not a tech-savvy person, you probably groaned when you read this chapter title. But never fear, creating a website for your book is not terribly difficult! In fact, it is fun and straightforward once you learn how.

You may want to create a website on your own, or you may want to hire someone to do it for you. That is your prerogative. However, you must have a website dedicated to your pet book. If you already have a website, that is great. What you will need to do is create a landing page for your book—just as you would for a service, event, etc.

You might think you do not need a website. But sadly, you are missing out on a huge market and great marketing opportunities. Creating a web presence is essential to helping you get the word out.

I created my own website with Wordpress and the Avada theme. I go into how you can do this in my first book in this series:

Pet Blogging 101: How to Start a Riveting Pet Blog and Gain Loyal Followers (https://amazon.com/dp/B07XWRS95W).

I won't go into the technical aspects here, as I want to focus on what you must include in your website. Please check out the Resources in the back of this book to help you out as well.

A Winning Author Website

First and foremost, your website is a form of marketing. You must treat it as such. The purpose of your site is to provide a place where readers can go to keep track of what you are publishing. A website is a tool where you make an impression, convince readers to read your book, and also tell people a bit about yourself.

You can create a site using your author name or the name of your book. I recommend going with your author name. Especially if you plan to write more books. Using the name of your book or series can be extremely limiting. However, if you write one book or a series—and that is all you plan to do—you can dedicate an entire site to either your one book or series title.

Feature an "About The Author" Page

This is where you talk about who you are. You include a biography and at least one picture of yourself. Pictures of your pets will sell even more copies! Try to show readers the image you want them to see and will best sell your book.

For example—a loving, compassionate veterinarian, a fierce opponent to habitat violation, a charming fiction writer. These are images your readers get from your books—depending on who you are. Uphold that image in your biography by sharing information with your readers. I talk a bit more about how to build a good biography in the "Amazon Author Central" section in this chapter.

Feature a Landing Page

This page shows your book cover, description, reviews, and where to buy it. You may include an Amazon link here. The purpose of this page is to convince people why your book is worth reading.

A landing page is a page on your website dedicated to your book. Creating a landing page for your book is a great idea if your book is part of your business. I have landing pages for all of my books on my websites:

- centerforpetlossgrief.com
- centerforanimalcommunication.com
- wendyvandepoll.com

For Center for Pet Loss Grief, LLC, my actual site is centered around the subject of pet loss grief. I feature a home page where I share the basic premise of the site and what users can expect. But I also have a clearly visible list of links at the top for my products. It makes it easy for people to enter my site, know what it is about, and navigate to what they need. Only people who need my resources are likely to visit my site. I market to them by showing how I can help them.

Nonfiction needs to sell the book by showing how readers will learn from it. Make the biggest promise that you can keep here.

Some examples:

"Are you at your wit's end trying to house-train your puppy? In my book, I offer a twelve-step system you can use to train your puppy in a week!"

"If you are debating about adding a snake to your family, you probably have many questions. I answer all of them and more in *There's a Snake in the House*! By the end of this book, you will have the confidence to purchase your first reptilian pet."

See how these promises are specific? They tell a reader what:

- The book is about
- They will learn
- Benefits they will gain
- Time frame they can expect to see those benefits

Meanwhile, fiction needs to include a power-packed description. Bryan Cohen's book, *How to Write a Sizzling Synopsis*, is another great one about creating descriptions especially for fiction. With your fiction, you want to share what the book is basically about, while leaving a lot of suspense in the reader's mind. I have found this book helps me write my nonfiction descriptions as well.

When you do this, the reader (your avatar from Chapter 2) is eager to buy it and find out how it ends. You want to create a brief description or even share a sample of the book that acts as a sort of teaser. If this book is part of a series, mention the series title and include what number in the series the book is.

Be sure to feature clear links to your book on your home page and a menu bar item that takes users to a landing page marketing your book.

Include a Contact Page

This page will include a contact form for people to contact you directly with questions. Have a sign-up form for people to subscribe to your emails. Include social media links to all of your social media profiles (which will be covered more in Chapter 15) and information about your pet business, if you have one.

This page is important, since readers may have questions or concerns after reading your book. Or they may have questions before they read it. By being available and open to chatting, you make them feel supported and inclined to become your biggest fans.

Always answer all emails and respond to comments on your site and social media accounts. If you cannot keep up with all of the emails you get, then consider hiring a virtual assistant (Glossary) to help you. Some email programs also automate your reply. An automation can let people know you received their email and will be responding soon.

Each person who visits your site is a potential lead, or customer. You want to sell your book to them. With that in mind, think how you can make your site stand out and entice people to read your book. Great critical reviews, photos of you signing your book at a big bookstore, and a tantalizing description will entice readers.

Feature a Blog

I believe it is necessary to have a blog as an author. Publishing books, especially on animals, is competitive. In a blog, you can post new and relevant things relating to your book.

For instance, if I write a *new* book about managing pet loss grief, I'll want to create a blog post about it. The article shares what the book is about, but also shares twenty percent of the book's secrets so readers want to buy it and learn the other eighty.

I'll also want to post other relevant content and articles about pet loss grief on my blog that does not have to do with my books. This strategy keeps people visiting my page and keeps me relevant in their minds.

Furthermore, it entices people to sign up for my email lists. I can send them free gifts, book announcements, and notifications that will get them to buy one of my books or other products.

The first book in this series, *Pet Blogging 101: How to Start a Riveting Pet Blog and Gain Loyal Followers* (https://amazon.com/dp/B07XWRS95W), goes into great detail about this topic.

SEO

To rank highly in searches and help people find your book, you must use search engine optimization, or SEO. I also covered this extensively in *Pet Blogging 101: How to Start a Riveting Pet Blog and Gain Loyal Followers,* but I will go over the basics here and in the Glossary.

It is easy to get buried in the mountains of content on the web. That is why you must utilize SEO. Throughout your content and site metadata (Glossary), you must include keywords that people are likely to search related to your book. To find these words, be sure to do some research.

Google Keyword Planner (Resources) is one of many ways that you can research keywords and find out the most popular, or high-ranking, ones. Use a mixture of high- and medium-ranking keywords (Glossary) throughout your website content and in the page and site descriptions. That way, people will find you.

Amazon Author Central

On top of having a website, you want to create an Amazon Author Central page (Resources). This page highlights who you are as an author and allows you to claim all books you have self-published on the Amazon platform. Readers can visit your profile and see your other books, if you have published more than one.

Amazon Author Central has a great help section, and the customer service crew is awesome and helpful. But I will sum it up in this section for you.

- Visit Amazon Author Central and sign up.
- The sign-up process is quite self-explanatory.
- You will want to claim your books on Amazon.
- Fill in all the options to inspire potential readers to buy your books.
- Finally, you want to post a profile picture and write a riveting biography.

For your profile picture, choose something that represents your love of animals. For dog books, you want to be posing with your beloved dog, for example. Make sure the photo is well lit from behind the camera and shows your face. Do not hide your face with sunglasses or a hat. A smile is most inviting, but you can also wear a serious expression if that is your brand.

For your biography, share something that makes people feel connected to you and able to trust your knowledge. If you are a licensed veterinarian with a specialty in exotic animals, for instance, be sure to say so. If you run a rescue, tell people why you do this type of work. You want pet owners to read your biography and think, "Wow, this person is someone I can relate to and trust on the subject of pets."

You also want to seem like a real person. You want to talk a bit about yourself. Include:

- Where you are from
- Where you went to college
- If you are married
- How many kids you might have
- Talk about your pets and how many
- List your hobbies

- Talk about foreign countries you may have lived in or visited
- Share what you do for a living
- Reveal some of your passions

Think of what makes you unique and human, then add to your Author Central biography. When you present yourself as a real person, you can allow readers to connect more with you.

For example, I include fun facts like:

1. As a wolf biologist, I was followed by a wild wolf in minus sixty below weather.
2. When walking my dog, Addie, I was hissed at by a wild bobcat.
3. Hiking with Marley one morning, I was huffed and chased by a momma bear.

What if you have other books that are not pet-related?

There are a few ways to go about this. The simplest way is to publish all of your books under one name and feature them on your page. Give a general biography that touches on your expertise in all areas of the subjects you write about.

If you write fiction, talk about where you are from, what you do for a living, and maybe if you have a family or pets, as well as anything interesting about yourself. A fun fact is not a bad idea to include as well.

But you can also publish in different genres under different names. Your nonfiction pet books might be under your real name, while your romance is under a pseudonym, or vice versa. You can create different pages for each name in Author Central, claim the books you publish under each name, and then link them so that you can access and control them all from one account. There is no need to create multiple Amazon Central accounts.

Be sure to update your biography as soon as changes occur in your life. You can use these biographies as "About the Author" sections on your books and update them with each new release. You should also feature this biography on your website. The same biography creates consistency so that people remain sure you are the same person.

Wrap-Up

A web presence is essential for any author. You can build a site yourself or hire someone to do it for you. Be sure to feature your book prominently on a landing page on your site and also on social media.

A blog is an effective tool to promote your book. You can reference your publication within a blog article, send potential customers to Amazon to purchase, and also grow your mailing list by offering a free gift in exchange for an email.

I have found many authors do not make use of their Author Central account. This is a wonderful resource to gain followers, clients, and/or book purchasers. This platform is free and is instrumental to your success as an author. Be sure to fill out all the options. Do not leave anything blank. You want your visitors to become followers and purchase your books.

Are you ready to get your book out there? Then read on to start building your launch team. Treat your team well and they will help create interest for your book! But first, check out your action steps for this chapter so you are well prepared.

Action Steps

1. Create a website yourself or hire someone to do it for you.
2. Include an engaging biography and photos with you and your animals.
3. Create a landing page dedicated to your book(s).
4. Try blogging to gain followers and increase your visibility on Google.
5. Design an easy-to-understand contact page for people to get in contact with you.
6. Set up the SEO for your website and your landing pages.
7. Create an Amazon Author Central page and fill it out completely.
8. Keep your biography updated over time.

13

BUILD A LAUNCH TEAM

If you have a dream, do not just sit there. Gather courage to believe that you can succeed and leave no stone unturned to make it a reality.
— Dr. Roopleen

Have you ever heard of a launch team? Your launch team, also known as your street team, is a group of people who spread the word about your book and encourage others to buy it. They are your first step in marketing your book.

The great thing about your launch team is they can help you spread the word, get people excited about your book, and generate sales for you. Word of mouth is always the best and most trusted form of advertising, and your team can help.

Your launch team will accomplish this by:

- Downloading, reading, and writing reviews for your book on Amazon and other platforms

- Sharing your book to their following, friends, and family
- Creating and sharing social media posts with their following
- Hosting ads on their websites and blogs

They may also be able to put you in touch with major social media or publishing influencers. These platforms and/or folks can offer significant traffic to your book and website with their endorsements and reviews.

A huge part of launching your book is networking with other people. Other people can open up opportunities, provide marketing, and help spread the word for you. You do not have to do all of this work on your own—a great launch team can help you. When you communicate your expectations, educate, and stay in touch with them, your book will sell.

A launch team does not have to be made up of expensive professionals. Rather, it can consist of your friends, family, business followers, clients, and members of your local circle. It can include those who follow you on your author Facebook page and writer's groups. It can even include the employees of local pet businesses, libraries, and bookstores. Read on to learn about how to build a great launch team.

Encourage Word of Mouth

When you first get ready to publish your book for pet lovers and/or pet professionals, you should consider giving free copies to:

- People in the pet industry

- Your friends
- Local pet businesses
- Acquaintances, etc.

Ask these people to spread the word and recommend your book to others. Word of mouth will encourage many people to read your book who might not otherwise give it a chance.

Think About It

When you see a new restaurant open up in town, you might not give it a try unless a friend tells you, "It is really great food!" You do not want to risk wasting your time and money trying something unless someone you know and trust tells you that it is worth it. The same goes for your pet book. People may not read or consider it—unless they hear from trusted sources they should.

Another consideration is to launch your freshly published book with your own expanded social circle. People who know you are already more likely to share your interests and trust your book is worth reading. Then they will spread the word and share it with others they know who might like it. This is how your book starts to gain notoriety and sales.

Sadly, many people overlook this free form of easy marketing. They do not want to bother their friends and family by asking them to read their books. They feel shy or worry their close friends won't enjoy their books.

Take advantage of your friends, family, acquaintances, local pet businesses, and bookstores to help spread work of mouth for you. This marketing is free and also effective. You have vast resources at your fingertips at the local level if only you take advantage of them!

Early Access

Right after you upload your book to a self-publishing platform (Chapter 14), you absolutely should offer free or low-cost (I suggest $.99) Kindle copies to gain momentum in the Amazon algorithms (Glossary).

Your supporters can be the word-of-mouthers discussed above. But do not rely on your friends and family exclusively. You need social media influencers, pet bloggers, and avid Amazon book reviewers. When you reach out to them, in exchange for free or inexpensive access to your book, these people will spread the word and post reviews on your book.

By giving your book out, you incur the rule of reciprocity. People will hopefully feel obligated to do something for you in exchange for something you do for them. That way, you can ensure at least a few people actually read your book and leave reviews—directing other people to read it. Reviews will definitely boost sales.

Furthermore, if any of these people leave negative reviews early on, you can take their words as constructive feedback.

1. What did they not like about the book?
2. What could you improve?
3. Did you forget to include something?

Most often, negative book reviews are because the book was not clear, the book did not have good grammar, flow, and/or plotline. Or the book failed to address and/or provide what it promised it would. You can work on these things and then re-release the book.

You can also reach out to your followers on social media. Tell your followers that the first twenty, fifty, or hundred people to sign up for your newsletter will get a free copy of your book. Then you hope they give you a review.

Is this foolproof? No, it is not. You might send several people copies and never hear from them again—this is normal. While this can be disappointing, you will get some reviews to show for your efforts. Plus, you got your book into the hands of more people! This is a good thing.

Reviewers

Many professional book reviewers are admired and respected in their industry. People may not even become aware of books until they read reviews under popular columns and/or a popular reviewer.

A great form of marketing is to get such acclaimed critics to read your book and review it. You will reach many people this way, people who may never otherwise learn of your book's existence.

Look up bloggers and book reviewers in your particular pet industry and genre. Next, view their website and review policy. Book reviewers should have them clearly posted. If not, you may consider contacting the reviewer and politely introduce yourself, pitching the book in a few sentences, and asking how you can submit it for review.

Some reviewers want print copies, while others want ebooks. They will have rules about where and how to submit books, what to include with your submission, and even the dates when they accept new submissions.

Write the reviewer a personalized letter or email. You can create a form letter that you use again and again—be sure to tweak it for each reviewer. Address the reviewer by name and with a polite salutation. Do not waste time with words—be succinct and get to the point.

1. First, introduce yourself and state how you located the reviewer.
2. Then, launch into a brief description of your book, what it will do for readers, and why it is worth reading.
3. Finally, offer to send a free copy in the format the reviewer prefers and thank him or her for their time.
4. Sign it "Sincerely" and with your full name.
5. Before you send the letter or email off, be sure to proofread it. Errors look quite amateur and decrease your chances of hearing a response.
6. When a reviewer responds with interest in your book, be sure to send it promptly. Thank the reviewer again for taking the time to review your book.

As you collect reviews, be sure to share them on social media, Amazon Central, and post them on your site (with the reviewer's permission, of course!). The more attention and mention your book gets, the more people will feel comfortable reading it. The law of social proof means, if at least a few people read your book, then others will feel comfortable trying it out themselves.

Again, negative reviews may be hurtful or even crushing, but use them constructively to improve your book. Professional book reviewers are people with their own personal opinions—do not take every review to heart. Unless a critic offers some truly valuable advice on how to improve your book, or several people review it negatively for the same reasons, you do not need to follow the guidance of every negative review.

Definitely do not hold off on publishing your book just because of a negative review or two. Not everyone will love your book. This is a reality that comes with self-publishing. Writing scathing replies to negative reviewers may be tempting, but it will only make you look bad in the long run. Handle negative reviews with grace and move on.

Social Media Influencers

Social media influencers are people who have amassed hundreds of thousands of social media followers and use social media to promote products or brands for money. They have a huge platform and audience to market to, and they have access to many people who may read your book.

Find literary and pet influencers on social media. These would be pages and people who have thousands of followers and mostly promote books or pet products. Watch a few of their videos and read their posts to see what their approaches are. Then, reach out to them with personalized emails, inviting them to read and promote your book.

You can also try a marketing device like BookTweeters

(Resources). For a small fee, these services will post daily tweets about your book for a set period of time. They can place your book in front of the right readers and spread your marketing throughout the social media world for you.

Influential Endorsements

What are influential endorsements? They are the people in your pet community who have clout. They may include veterinarians, veterinary technicians, groomers, pet store owners, shelter owners, boarding kennel owners, competitive owners of show animals, judges, and the like. Check out my book, *Pet Jobs 101: How to Choose Your Dream Job and Thrive in the Pet Industry* (https://amazon.com/B08478KMYD), for a list of all potential influencers in the pet industry.

Celebrities are also excellent endorsements, if you can convince one to endorse your book. Even if you cannot get an A-list movie star to endorse your book, you can ask local celebrities, such as local news anchors or spokespeople for major local organizations. Bloggers in your area of pet expertise who have lots of followers are also excellent influential endorsements.

Reach out to influential people. You may visit them in person or write them letters. Always be direct and polite. Point out:

- Why your pet book is good
- What it is about
- How it will help pet owners in some way
- What you hope to accomplish with your book

This will convince influential people, who are probably busy, to take some time out of their day to promote your book somehow.

Find people who care about the same pet-related things you do. If you wrote a book about shelter dogs, for instance, you would want to find people who donate to or run shelters. If your book is about lizards, you would want to reach out to people who are well known among reptile owners—such as reptile product company owners or reptile store owners.

Wrap-Up

Gathering a launch team is a critical step in your self-publishing journey. Honestly, work on building your team before you publish (Chapter 13). Have your team prepped for the date your book is live on Amazon. The more preparation you do by following my advice, the more downloads and reviews you will get.

Keep in mind you will *not* get one-hundred percent participation from your team, but you will get about thirty percent activity. This is why you have to keep working on keeping your book prominent on social media (Chapter 15) and events (Chapter 16).

Your launch team will help get your book out there! You can turn to friends, book reviewers, local celebrities, clients, and business owners to get the word out. Never underestimate word of mouth! This is one way to market your book even before you release it to the public. Offer people free copies in exchange for word-of-mouth advertising.

There is a lot that goes into gathering a launch team, and it would take an entire book to explain the subject. The information in this chapter gives you a solid premise on what to gather, what you need, and what you can expect.

Now it is time to learn how to upload your book to Amazon. Read on to the next chapter to find out how to do that! But check out your action steps for this chapter first.

Action Steps

1. Encourage worth of mouth.
2. Get some early reviewers by offering free copies of your book.
3. Get influential endorsements.
4. Take advantage of a social media influencer's following.
5. Enter partnerships with other writers, bloggers, and pet business owners.
6. Collect book reviews to be posted on the day you launch by your launch team and to use on your Amazon Central page.
7. Be sure to use negative reviews constructively, and do not let them discourage you. Never respond to them on Amazon.

14

KINDLE DIRECT PUBLISHING

A professional writer is an amateur who did not quit.
— Richard Bach

Are you ready to hit publish? With your book edited, formatted, and with its cover designed, you now need to upload your book to a self-publishing platform. The one I use and strongly recommend is Kindle Select, which puts your book in the Kindle Unlimited store (if you so choose).

Being part of Kindle Direct Publishing allows users to find your book when they search for your book's subject on search engines and within the Amazon site. As long as you completely fill out the options for your book—keywords, description, etc.

If you do not already use Kindle Unlimited yourself, it is a massive ebook store where users pay a monthly fee to get access to hundreds of thousands of titles.

You can pick a book in the Kindle Unlimited program and download it to your Kindle app on any supporting device. Kindle is the current trend in self-publishing and lets you get your book in front of millions of users.

Amazon gives you the option to place your book in Kindle Select or not. I highly suggest you do because Amazon will promote your book. At least enroll for the first three months of publication. Kindle Select allows you to run promotions within the platform. Because of the scope of this information, I suggest going into KDP and learn more about Kindle Select and Unlimited.

But let's get your book published. Read on to find out what you need to do to become a self-published author.

Create a Kindle Direct Publishing Account

To upload, you first need to create a Kindle Direct Publishing (KDP) account. Go to https://kdp.amazon.com. The platform in KDP is extremely easy, and they also have a help section and an easy-to-reach customer service department.

Note: I recommend you sign up with KDP using a different username/email and password than the one you use if you already have a personal Amazon account. I like to have two separate accounts because it keeps my business history separate from my personal buying history. This makes tax time easier.

Time to Upload

Now you are ready to upload!

1. Sign in to your KDP account.
2. Click on your "Bookshelf."
3. Click on "Create a New Title."
4. Click on "Kindle ebook."
5. Select "Kindle ebook Details" and fill out *everything*.
6. Next, go to "Kindle ebook Content" and follow the prompts.
7. Then save and continue, and proceed to "Kindle ebook Pricing."
8. Be sure to fill out *everything*—and refer to the detailed help section in KDP.

Important Considerations

When you choose "Upload ebook Manuscript." It will pull up a window of your computer files, so locate your manuscript and select it. Hit "Open." It can take a few minutes, but you will receive a confirmation your book is uploaded. Next, you want to preview the book to ensure nothing went wrong.

You can also repeat this process when KDP provides a pop-up to create a print version. You can offer the same book in both ebook and print if you want. Follow the directions as you did above.

When you are asked to proof your book, definitely order an author's proof for a softcover. You want to be sure your softcover book is perfect. I covered formatting and cover design in Chapter 11; please go back and review if needed.

Be sure you have your softcover and your digital cover formatted to KDP's specifications. I always get an author's copy because it is so much easier to check a book in print format than on the computer screen. Plus, Amazon does make mistakes.

Definitely do some keyword research using Google Keyword Planner or a similar service to find keywords people might use when looking for books like yours. You want people to find your book easily. Do not skip this step.

To set the price, you first must pick a royalty plan. After you choose your royalty plan you will then set pricing. You will be given a list of currency options and the ability to set your desired amount.

Be sure to specify in your Kindle account how you want to receive your royalties. Also, learn the royalties schedule so you know when to expect payment. You will need to file for an EIN (Resources) and report your royalty earnings to the IRS.

After your book is live, you want to sign in to your Amazon Author Central and click "Add Book." Search by your book's title or ISBN. When you find it, hit "Claim." That adds the book to your list! You can refresh the page, and it should be on your page. You also want to post links to the book on your website and social media so people can start buying it!

This whole process is free! And it puts your book in front of countless readers. Your only job left is marketing.

Wrap-Up

Launching your book after all the work you put into it is an exciting feeling when self-publishing—especially the first time. It is the ultimate accomplishment, the moment when you can honestly say, "I am an author!" With Kindle Direct Publishing, or KDP, self-publishing is easier than ever. Just follow the directions KDP offers.

Familiarize yourself with the KDP platform. Read the helpful articles that are available to you in KDP's help section. Although this process can be stressful—uploading your pet book to KDP gets easier with each book you publish.

Be sure to have your manuscript formatted correctly (a professional formatter makes this part so much easier) and your cover properly designed to fit the template that KDP provides. I recommend a professional cover designer as well.

Upload the ebook and/or print versions and fill out the relevant information. Pick a royalty plan and set a price for your new book. Then watch the reviews and earnings flow in! Do not forget to claim the book on your Amazon Author Central account (Chapter 12).

This is not the last step, however. First do your action steps for this chapter. Then go to the next chapter and learn how to get more reviews and increase your earnings. Continued marketing of your book is critical.

In the next two chapters, I cover the basic yet crucial forms of marketing you must do to sell your book. After all, no one can read your book if no one knows it is out there!

Action Steps

1. Make sure your manuscript is properly edited and formatted (Chapter 11).

2. Get your cover design .jpg finalized to fit the template that KDP requires.
3. Create a KDP account.
4. Upload your ebook and print versions.
5. Fill out *all* the book details—do not skimp.
6. Pick your royalty plan.
7. Set your price and currency.
8. Preview to make sure it looks right.
9. Order your author copy for the softcover.
10. Alert your launch team to download and leave their reviews (Chapter 13).
11. Read on to start marketing your creation to pet lovers, influencers, and professionals.

15

INTERNET MARKETING

*Content is King, but engagement is Queen, and
the Queen rules the house!*
—Mari Smith

Are you ready to influence the pet industry with your message? Since many folks are online these days, it makes sense to market your book using social media. You will reach a wider and possibly international audience with Internet marketing. It is possible to build a huge following and get many readers with the right kinds of channels.

The first thing you must do is establish yourself on social media. What are the most popular ones in your area and/or for your brand? Twitter, Instagram, LinkedIn, and Facebook are the big ones right now. If you do not sign up for any other social media, at least sign up for those four.

Chances are you are already on social media, but you want to keep your author accounts and personal accounts separate.

That protects your privacy and lets you market to the right audiences. Read on to learn how to take advantage of these sites for marketing purposes.

Facebook

Facebook is huge all over the world, and many businesses have used this platform to their advantage. You definitely want to create a business page for yourself as an author. This will begin your strategy for the online promotion process.

Your business page is your headquarters, with statistics about audience engagement, easy access to ad creation and posting, and a means to post new content.

You can also pay Facebook to promote your page. This is where Facebook places your page ad in front of people who have liked related pages in the past and thus are likely to like yours. As you incur likes, you will grow a wider base of people to put content in front of.

Another great thing about Facebook—you can join groups related in some way to your book. It is a great way to find people who will read your book. You can engage through thoughtful comments and let people see your page name. They will then be more inclined to check out your page, like it, share it, and hopefully buy your book.

Start by inviting your friends and family on your personal Facebook to like your page. Ask them to invite their friends and family. As they invite more and more people, you begin to grow a decent fanbase of people who have never even met you before. They are new potential leads for your book.

Post content every day. About twenty percent of your content should actually be about your book. You can post:

- Blurbs
- Book deals
- Reviews
- Promotional deals
- Upcoming appearances on local cable television news
- And more

But the rest of your content should be relevant and interesting—providing equal parts of informative and entertainment value.

You can also post some funny memes, a few cute animal videos, and then a couple insightful articles about canine nutrition and/or behavior to inspire users to keep following you. Post engaging content that is fun, educational, and relevant to your book and/or brand (Glossary).

Instagram

Instagram is about posting great photos. You may think this would be difficult to translate into promotional material for your book, but you can definitely use your creativity to market using this platform.

Here are examples of the types of posts I do. Depending on your genre, you can post photos of your:

- Own pets or pet products
- Followers and influencer interacting with your book(s)

- Pets alongside of your book(s)
- Newest articles on your blog
- And other relevant things that entertain and educate

With over seven hundred million users on Instagram, it is the most popular social media site right now. You would be missing out if you weren't on it! Instagram marketing is powerful.

Start by setting up an Instagram business page. Your business page could be specifically for your book (not my recommendation, as you may write more books in the future), or better yet—you as an author.

Use your page's built-in insights to understand your audience better. Remember, insights only come with business pages, not regular personal pages. Be sure to utilize them to create ads that work, posts that get more likes, and allow visitors to contact you directly.

A thirty/thirty-five/thirty-five rule is ideal for Instagram. Thirty percent of your posts should be promoting your book. Thirty-five percent should be educational (educational links to blog posts and insightful videos, for instance) and thirty-five percent should be to entertainment (cute puppy videos, for instance).

Be sure to post every day. And avoid those glaringly artificial stock photos. Take your own photos if you can. Nice mobile photos of your pets may not look polished and professional—but they do look refreshingly real. Instagrammers appreciate that! Be sure to engage with your commenters and thank them for checking out your stuff.

Be sure to use hashtags (Glossary). A hashtag is a keyword phrase without spaces with a pound sign in front of it. For example: #petauthorpreneur, #petloss, #petsofinstagram. I cover hashtags in more detail in the Glossary and in my book, *Pet Blogging 101: How to Start a Riveting Pet Blog and Gain Loyal Followers* (https://amazon.com/dp/B07XWRS95W).

To get followers, you must be a follower. Follow the people you admire, like other authors or pet business owners. Engage with their content so they notice you. Following those with pages related to yours can help you grow and expand your followers by putting you in line with people who will like your content.

Twitter

To use Twitter as a marketing strategy, you want to tweet something at least once a day. This helps readers feel connected to you. You might tweet a sentence from your book, a quote about pets, and or a quote about writing—always add a link to your book. Tweet when you are appearing in:

- An ad
- A critical review
- A podcast
- Or some other online or in-person event so your readers can attend

Always provide links and hashtags (Glossary) to whatever you are talking about—be it your book or a podcast you will be a guest on.

Twitter posts move fast. Therefore, create captivating copy that is short, to the point, and fast to read. When you provide great information in a concise and captivating manor, it increases the odds your tweets will be retweeted. Your efforts will reach a broader audience and earn you more followers. Quotes or short teasers are also ideal.

When someone shares your tweet, be sure to thank him or her. This can be time-consuming. But it helps you stand out from the crowd and incur loyal fans who feel valued by you. The more personal interaction you have with your readers, the better.

An especially good move on Twitter is to befriend and talk to people whom you want to get to know. You can make a list of famous people, pet lovers, business owners, authors—and then follow them. Once you get to know them, you can glean helpful information from them. They may even retweet your posts about your book and spread the word to an even larger group of people!

You should also be helpful to others. Retweet their books. Post links to articles and products other authors and pet lovers could appreciate or use. These things make people feel as if you are worth following.

It is best to use the 4:1 rule here. For every four things you post that are helpful or useful, post one thing that promotes your book. This keeps followers from unfollowing you. You do not want them to get tired of reading about your book and nothing else. Most people do not enjoy monotony or being spammed (Glossary)! Especially on social media, where trends fade in and out within days of each other.

Every so often, you should host Tweet chats where you chat directly with your readers and future readers. Create a hashtag specific to your chat and then encourage readers to use it during the event. Clearly post hours and be present for it. This is a chance for you to talk about your book and answer questions.

LinkedIn

LinkedIn is a social networking site for professionals. To promote your pet book business—definitely create a LinkedIn profile. On the profile, talk about your expertise and feature a link to your book(s).

As you add new followers, be sure to send an email greeting to each new member by name and then invite them to look at your book(s). Talk about what your book features and how they will benefit from following you.

It helps to create a basic email template. Copy and paste it to each new email you send out. Customize the name, and you are good to go.

Post every day or every other day. Talk about your book, blog posts, or a book event you will be attending. This way, LinkedIn users can follow your book launches.

As with all social media platforms, add a LinkedIn button on your website to your book Landing Page, About Page, and Contact Page (Chapter 12).

AMS Ads

Amazon Market Services, or AMS, ads are a great way to drive people to your book on Amazon with little effort on your part. Go to https://advertising.amazon.com to set up your account.

The key to AMS ads is to first research keywords (Glossary) and gather the maximum of one thousand words that will do well according to your SEO (Glossary) research. Then create an ad with Amazon and enter a clear description—Amazon will pull an image from your book listing. As a beginner, set a bid for ten cents per click and a cap of two dollars a day.

It takes time and knowledge to build successful AMS ads, and I would need to write an entire book on the strategy. Plus, Amazon is always changing the way they do things. I love and recommend Bryan Cohen's book and course on creating AMS ads (Resources). You could also purchase Publisher Rocket (Resources), which is an app you can download.

Keep in mind as you set up your ads—clicks cost you money, so you want them to lead to sales. If you are getting a lot of unproductive clicks, perhaps improve your book description or your keywords. Review your keyword traffic and eliminate the words that seem to be getting the most unresponsive clicks. Unresponsive clicks are part of the business, so you will get some, but do your best to avoid them.

Great Place to Find Keywords

You know the list of books that appear under any book on Amazon, "Customers who bought this item also bought..." This is a great place to find relevant keywords.

The way to do this is to take a look at each book. Ask yourself, "Are these books bestsellers, have great ratings, have over fifty reviews?" If so, add the title and the author's name as a separate keyword in your list of available one thousand words.

When you do this, you are treating authors in your genre and niche who are bestsellers as potential leads for clicks and hopefully sales. When you show up in the "Customers who bought this item also bought..." recommendations, readers will then likely click on your book, buy it, and hopefully leave a review.

Wrap-Up

The Internet is a fantastic place to put your book in front of many people. On top of a website (Chapter 12) and a launch team (Chapter 13), you must use AMS ads and social media to build your brand and sell your book.

I always recommend designing a plan when you are developing your social media strategy. Having a plan and checklist can keep you accountable for creating new posts, engaging with your followers, and general marketing of your brand and books.

Your goal as an author is to gain loyal followers. Social media will help you collect emails, inspire people to buy your book(s), and engage with you.

Be sure to give pet lovers, influencers, and professionals great content so they are loyal to your brand. Your posts cannot be *all* about your book! Be sure to post at least three or four posts that entertain and/or educate before you try to convince them to buy your book(s).

Even though there is a learning curve with AMS ads, do not delay in starting the process as soon as you are live on Amazon. Check out Bryan Cohen's book and course. If you are patient and do your research, your ads can be extremely profitable.

Go over your action steps below to help you with your strategy for online marketing. The next and final chapter is about the old-fashioned way of self-promotion—in-person marketing. This approach is an effective way to put your book in front of new readers who might enjoy it or need it.

Action Steps

1. Set up a business Facebook author page.
2. Set up a business Instagram account.
3. Set up a Twitter business account.
4. Set up a LinkedIn account.
5. Decide which day(s) you are going to post on your accounts.
6. Engage with followers and the people you follow on a daily basis.
7. Find people you can follow with all four accounts.
8. Join Facebook groups.
9. Start a Twitter chat.
10. Sign up for AMS ads by going to https://advertising.amazon.com, do your research, and watch closely—you have to pay attention to your AMS ads.

16

IN PERSON MARKETING

You cannot expect to just write and have visitors come to you—that is too passive.
—Anita Campell

Are you concerned that Internet marketing is the only way to promote your book? As popular as the Internet is—meeting people in person and forging personal relationships is still an effective way to market your book.

When people meet you in person, they feel connected to you and are more likely to read your book. You are not a faceless, anonymous stranger selling your book online—instead, you are a real person who makes a certain impression.

But how do you accomplish this and go out in public to promote your book? There are actually a few simple and fun events I want to share with you. These options are excellent ways to show people the real you and raise awareness of your book. Garner the attention and interest, make an impression, and sell your book with these public appearances.

Book Signings

One of the best ways to raise interest in your book is to go on a book tour. With a book tour, you make in-person appearances at bookstores and libraries. It gives you a chance to interact with people by offering book signings.

In traditional publishing, your literary agent will set you up to do this. In self-publishing, you have to set it up for yourself. But it is worth it and not as hard as it may sound!

You may consider only local businesses or those in cities that you will visit soon. The first thing to do is to locate:

- Bookstores
- Pet supply stores
- Shelters
- Pet events or fairs
- Pet bazaars
- Local community colleges
- And other places that would attract the types of people who would read your book (remember your avatar from Chapter 2)

Then, approach these locations several months in advance to give them time to accept your proposal and promote you. You will pitch the store owner or event/festival planner. If there is an upcoming event or festival, see if you can fit in a reading or presentation during it.

Keep in mind your host must see the worth of your book for their customers before hosting you. Be sure to immediately state in your proposal something of value to their customers.

Try and get your book on the shelves prior to your visit to a bookstore or library. This can help with promotion and marketing ahead of time. It can also decrease your luggage load if you are traveling a distance.

When you set up a signing, be sure to run an ad in the paper and on social media. Have the store post signs and mention it in their newsletter to generate more interest. Pin up notices in other local businesses with their permission. Definitely mention it on your author website. You want to spread the word.

What if your first book signing is a bit of a sad affair? No worries—I have suffered through many book signings where people weren't interested. This is no reason to give up. Keep posting about it and sharing photos of your books. This is a great use of your time when your event is a flop. Keep in mind the event still:

- Gives you material to post on your social media
- Assures people your books are being read
- Gives you social proof

Podcasts

Even though a podcast is not technically an in-person event, they are extremely helpful, and I wanted to include them in this chapter.

A podcast is another fantastic and fun way to get people to follow you and buy your book(s). You do not have to start your own podcast—although it certainly is not a bad idea! Rather, you want to find related podcasts that will have you on as a guest to talk about your book and your pet business. The podcaster will interview you, and you will get to share a bit about why your book is worth buying.

It is useful to listen to podcasts in your field of pet expertise and find the ones you want to be on. Reach out to the podcaster with a personal letter and pitch explaining why you are a great guest for their listeners.

You want to show your host the value of your message for their listeners. Before you go live, you also want to prepare some material. This way, when you get nervous you won't forget what you wanted to say (trust me, it happens to the best of us!).

Be sure to alert people to your upcoming podcast interviews on your social media and website. This lets users tune in and boost the podcast's listeners. This way, you give the podcaster something in return for the great marketing and promotional opportunity you got from him or her.

Some podcasters are happy to interview over the Internet or phone. Others will want to meet in person. Look into how the interview will take place to make sure it fits into your schedule.

Book Groups

Also try out a book group as a chance to promote your pet

book. Book groups are groups of people who love books and often love to host authors. They can also offer honest and helpful reviews (Chapter 13).

Some book clubs meet in person, while others are members of Internet clubs. Your best bet is to find local and regional book clubs and learn when they meet. Contact the club's president and convince him or her to let you present your book during a club meeting.

Like a book signing, you will set up a table with several copies of your book. You will present your book for a few minutes to the club and then answer questions for a few minutes. You will sign copies as you distribute them to the club members. You will charge whatever you have priced your print copies at on Amazon.

The beauty of these clubs is the members like to read. While only a few may buy your book at your actual presentation, they may tell their friends about it. You can easily get expanded sales from just five attendees at a book club meeting.

If a book club loves your book and presentation, they will welcome you back if you write anything else. You have an easy source of promotion and word-of-mouth marketing at the same book club for the length of your author career!

If you cannot find a book club that is keen on your nonfiction or fiction pet book, you can try to reach out to other types of pet clubs. If you wrote a book about sheep herding, meet with a group of sheep herding trial competitors, for instance.

You can also look into online groups. You may want to post a video or use a live function on Facebook to present your book to the group. Post a link to your book on Amazon and watch the sales increase!

Do not forget your pets are an excellent source of promotion! Attend pet events with your book and your companions. This is a great way to get people to meet you and learn you are a trustworthy voice on the subject of pets.

Pet Specialty Groups and Events

As a pet author, this audience is priceless and not to be ignored. Rescue organizations, breed-specific groups, and/or training groups oftentimes host fundraising events to support their cause. Research the groups in your area first—in my experience, the local groups love to support other local people.

When I find a group or event that is promising, I reach out to the director with a brief email. I explain who I am, what I do, and provide the links to my website and book(s) on Amazon. At the beginning of my email, I explain the benefit to their members of having me at their event or group meeting in two sentences.

For my books, I have found this to be one of the most successful ways to market and gain loyal followers, reviews, and future buyers of my books and services.

Wrap-Up

Do not ever underestimate the power of marketing in person! People will love to meet you and learn what inspired you. This alone can help with sales because potential customers are experiencing a real person.

Start making a list for appearances on podcasts, bookstores for signings, book clubs, pet specialty groups, and events to promote your book and raise sales. All of these venues are perfect for authors.

Keep in mind, people love local authors and are usually enthusiastic about hosting you at an event. There are probably a good number of pet events in your area where you could show up to do a book signing.

You have now reached the end of this book—but not the end of your new journey as an author. You have many years of success ahead of you. While the work may never truly end, the rewards do not either.

You will love the sense of accomplishment you will feel from having written your book, and you will love the way your book can earn you a great income while you lounge at home in your pajamas.

I believe in you. Now believe in yourself! Apply the tools in this book and you will not regret it! But do not forget your action steps for this chapter and my Pep Talk in the next section!

Action Steps

1. Make a list of all bookstores, pet supply stores, libraries, pet specialty clubs, events, and festivals in your area.
2. Arrange book signings, talks, and personal book sales.
3. Research and reach out to podcasters. Some will want to meet and record you in person—others will not.

4. Become a special guest at local book clubs and be available for questions.
5. Get featured on online book clubs as well—like Facebook live book clubs, etc.

PEP TALK!

If writing has been on your list of things to accomplish for years, *yet* you did not have a clue on how to start—*now* you have the tools to create a winning, best-selling pet book.

There is no need to wait or procrastinate any longer. It is time to jump in and make your dream come true. Most people want to write—you will be one of the few who actually does!

Writing in the pet genre can be daunting and even scary at first. But as you can see after reading this book, the entire process is fairly straightforward, exciting, and life-changing. Just take your time, set reasonable and specific goals, and celebrate your achievements.

A good team is the single best way you can accomplish your goal without failure. A team motivates you and helps bring your book to fruition. Find good, reliable people to edit, design, and format your book before you complete your rough draft.

You must also use a great launch team. Your best friend or local pet store can be a part of your launch team. There is no need to spend a fortune on securing an expensive publicist. You can market yourself online, in person, and through word of mouth.

Were you worried about sales? Now you know how to boost sales with the tools in this book to raise awareness about your book(s) for pet lovers and professionals. Remember, no matter how great your book is, no one will buy it if they do not know about it! Get out there and share it.

Furthermore, do not shy away from creating a website. A website markets your book while you are asleep, eating, or away on vacation. With a few simple steps, like social media marketing and SEO, you can ensure that your website drives sales and coverts visitors into leads. You must have a web presence to survive in the literary industry these days.

Self-publishing is hard work, and it can be expensive, but you do not have to go into debt to accomplish your dream. You will certainly love being an author. Sharing your knowledge and passion is a heartwarming feeling.

How could it not be—you get to write about the best topic ever: pets!

I believe you can do this and reach your goals. You just need to believe in yourself, learn as much as you can, and put yourself out there.

At first, I struggled with self-doubt about becoming a successful Pet Authorpreneur. I was petrified when I wrote my first book. I kept asking myself, *Will anyone be interested in what I have to say? Will my books find their way into readers' hands?*

My first review on Amazon secured I was on the right track, and I reached my goal for becoming an author. I wanted to help people, and this one book led into over a dozen best-selling books and counting.

Get *ready* for your journey. Do not forget to *set* your goals and plan for success. Then write every day to get your book done.

You can do this! I believe in you!

Warmly,

Wendy Van de Poll

January 1, 2020

All books in The Pet Biz Series

- Pet Blogging 101: How to Start a Riveting Pet Blog and Gain Loyal Followers, (Book 1) - https://amazon.com/dp/B07XWRS95W
- Pet Jobs 101: How to Choose your Dream Job and Jumpstart Your Business. (Book 2) - https://amazon.com/dp/B08478KMYD
- Pet Authorpreneur 101: How to Become a Successful Pet Author and Grow Your Business, (Book 3) - https://amazon.com/dp/

GLOSSARY

Affiliate Links — Or affiliate marketing is a marketing strategy in which one business rewards another business (affiliate) for each visitor and/or purchase by that visitor. It is up to the affiliate to market. A special link is provided by the company the affiliate is promoting.

Amazon Algorithms — A complicated system by Amazon. Their layers of algorithms determine how books are ranked in the best-seller charts, popularity list, which books appear in the keyword search and the order in which they appear.

Avatar — Your avatar is like a real person—they have a name and family status. They live in a particular place and have hopes and dreams. An avatar is a detailed profile of your ideal customer. The avatar focuses on one person and outlines everything about them.

Back Matter — The book elements that occur in the back of your book after your body of work. Includes acknowledgements, appendix, glossary, resources, bibliography, references, illustration credits, and index.

Backstory for a Character — Basically the history of a fictional character. Their experiences that help to explain their desires, fears, motivations, etc.

Beta Reader — A person who reads a work of fiction before it is published and suggests improvements. They are not editors.

Branding — The marketing practice of creating a name and logo that identifies your product from others. A great brand strategy gives your business a major edge in a competitive market. It is your promise to your customers' needs.

Character Profile — A detailed description of a fictional character's life and personality. A quality character profile helps the author get into the mind of the character and make them come alive for readers.

Front Matter — The elements that occur in the front of your book prior to the body of your work. Includes series title page, title page, copyright page, dedication, epigraph, table of contents, list of illustrations, foreword, introduction, and abbreviations.

Google Keyword Planner — A tool that provides keyword ideas and traffic estimates to help you build traffic to your website.

Hashtags — A hashtag is a label for content. It helps others who are interested in a certain topic find content on that same topic. A hashtag looks something like this: #wendyvandepoll or #dogsoninstagram. Hashtags are used mostly on social media sites. They rocketed to fame on Twitter.

High Ranking Keyword — When your chosen keyword on your website or in your blog article ranks with Google on the first search page.

Keyword/ Short-tailed Keyword — Short tail keywords are search phrases with only one or two words. Their length makes them less specific than searches with more words. "Pet" (one word) is an example of a short tail keyword, whereas "holistic raw cat food" (four words) is a long tail keyword.

Long-tailed Keyword/ Keyword Phrase — A

keyword phrase is two or more words typed as a search query. For example, "What is the best way to feed my senior cat" is a good example of a keyword phrase.

Manuscript — This is essentially the earliest draft of your book. It is unpublished and the document that gets submitted to editors.

Medium Ranking Keyword — Same as a high ranking keyword but your chosen keyword may not be on the first page. More commonly found on the second page of a Google search.

Metadata — Is a series of micro-communications between your website and search engines. It lives and works behind the scenes in the HTML of web pages. It drives search engine optimization or SEO (see SEO).

Mind Map — A mind map is a visual representation of writing prompts that includes a central idea surrounded by connected branches of associated topics/chapters/characters/plots, etc.

Plot Hole — An inconsistency in the narrative or character development of your fiction manuscript.

Premise — In fiction it is the foundation of your story or the underlying idea of your story. It is the foundation that supports your entire plot.

SEO — SEO or Search Engine Optimization is the name given to an activity that attempts to improve search engine rankings. In search results Google™ displays links to pages it considers optimal according to your keywords.

Spammed — Is when you send your email subscribers too

many emails advertising for them to buy your product. You must send email that educate your readers to give them value rather than trying to sell them all the time.

Tautology — Writing the same thing twice in different words.

Virtual Assistant – An independent contractor who provides administrative services to clients while operating outside of the client's office. They are able to do social media management, the management of appointments and calendars, sending and answering emails, etc.

Working Title – Also known as a production title or tentative title. Basically, it is a temporary title used during the development of writing your manuscript.

Writer's Block – Is when an author loses the ability to produce new work, or experiences a creative slowdown. The issue ranges from difficulty in coming up with original ideas of being unable to produce work for a certain time period.

RESOURCES

A FREE GIFT

A Winning Checklist
~ Become a Successful Pet Author and
Grow Your Business ~

Here is your link to download:
https://wendyvandepoll.com/pet-authorpreneur-free-checklist

AFFILIATE SITES**

ConvertKit - email provider
https://wendyvandepoll.com/convert-kit

Kylitics
https://wendyvandepoll.com/k-lytics

ProWritingAid - editing software
https://wendyvandepoll.com/pro-writing-aid

Self-Publishing School – self-publish your book platform
https://wendyvandepoll.com/self-publishing-school

Siteground - website host
https://wendyvandepoll.com/siteground

AMAZON LINKS

Amazon Author Central
https://authorcentral.amazon.com

Kindle Direct Publishing (KDP)
https://kdp.amazon.com

ASSOCIATIONS

Editorial Freelancers Association
https://www.the-efa.org

International Association of Professional Book Editors
https://iapcollege.com

National Association of Independent Writers and Editors
https://naiwe.com

GRAPHIC DESIGN SITES

Canva
https://canva.com

PicMonkey
https://picmonkey.com

MARKETING

BookTweeters
https://literatureandlatte.com/scrivener/overview

PHOTOS

Deposit Photos
https://depositphotos.com

Librestock
https://librestock.com

Pixabay
https://pixabay.com

SERVICES

99designs
https://99designs.com

Fiverr
http://fiverr.com

Guru
https://guru.com

Smashwords (Also known as Mark's List)
https://smashwords.com/list

Upwork
https://upwork.com

Vistaprint
https://vistaprint.com

SOCIAL MEDIA ORGANIZATIONAL TOOLS

Agora Pulse
https://agorapulse.com

Buffer
https://buffer.com

Hootsuite
https://hootsuite.com

Later
https://later.com

ShareCount
https://www.sharedcount.com

WRITING COURSES

Writer's Digest
https://writersdigest.com

Writer's Write
https://writerswrite.com

Udemy
https://udemy.com/course/writing-with-flair-how-to-become-an-exceptional-writer

WRITING CHALLENGES

12 Short Stories in 12 months
https://writerswrite.co.za

NaNoWriMo
https://nanowrimo.org

NaPoWriMo
https://napowrimo.net

StoryADay
https://storyaday.org

Word of the Day
https://wordofthedaychallenge.wordpress.com

WRITING TOOLS

ProWritingAid (affiliate)
https://wendyvandepoll.com/pro-writing-aid

Scapple
https://literatureandlatte.com/scrivener/overview

Scrivner

https://literatureandlatte.com/scrivener/overview

Vellum
https://vellum.com

OTHER

Best Page Forward (Bryan Cohen)
https://bestpageforward.com

EIN or Employee Identification Number
https://www.irs.gov/businesses/small-businesses-self-employed/apply-for-an-employer-identification-number-ein-online

Google Keyword Planner
https://ads.google.com/home/tools/keyword-planner

Publisher Rocket
https://publisherrocket.com

Download your FREE GIFT!

A Success Checklist to Become a Successful Pet Author and Grow Your Business

https://wendyvandepoll.com/pet-authorpreneur-free-checklist

**The recommended sites are products that I use and highly recommend. They are affiliate links which means if you purchase the product, I receive a small commission (which helps me greatly as an author.) You are not charged more because of the affiliate link.

ACNOWLEDGEMENTS

I would like to thank all the animals who have trusted me to be their advocate and voice. They inspire me to be the best human-being I possibly can.

Many thanks go to my followers, students, and clients. Thank you for pushing me to write this book and others to follow in this series. It takes a team to put together a book and I would like to extend my appreciation to all that have helped along the way.

A huge hug goes to my husband, Rick. He is a remarkable animal lover and human being who dedicates his life to the animals and the environment. He inspires my soul. You can find his books on Amazon, as well.

ABOUT THE AUTHOR

Animals are Wendy Van de Poll's passion. Any chance she gets she is hiking with her dog, observing wildlife in her backwoods, and listening to their wisdom.

Wendy Van de Poll is an award-winning and International best-selling author of thirteen books and counting. She has been working with animals in various capacities for over forty years. With her success she is passionate about helping others achieve their writing and pet business goals.

Wendy has helped people around the world start their own blogging sites, pet businesses, and write best-selling books. Her clients describe Wendy as a "dedicated partner who helps get your ideas down on paper, your work (blog, job, or book) done, and in the hands of readers and customers who want more."

She is the founder of the CenterforPetLossGrief.com. Her website and blog provide a safe place for dedicated pet parents and pet professionals who want support and guidance with pet loss grief, hospice for pets, and coping with the loss of their pets.

Wendy is a certified end-of-life and grief coach and a tested animal communicator and medium.

She holds a Master of Science degree in wolf ecology and behavior and has run with wild wolves in Minnesota, coyotes in Massachusetts, and foxes in her backyard.

Wendy also coaches people who want write their own books about their pets and other topics.

Her articles can be seen on Medium.com as well as her own websites.

Her articles can be seen on:

Wendy Van de Poll, Bestselling Author, Influencer, Animal Advocate: https://wendyvandepoll.com

Center For Pet Loss Grief, LLC: https://centerforpetloss-grief.com

Medium.com: https://medium.com/@wendyvandepoll

Click Here to Get Your Free Gift
https://wendyvandepoll.com/pet-authorpreneur-free-checklist

Follow Wendy on Social Media

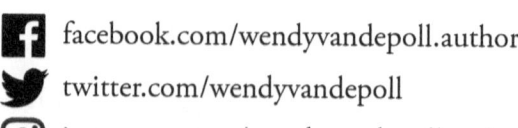

facebook.com/wendyvandepoll.author

twitter.com/wendyvandepoll

instagram.com/wendyvandepoll.author

Pet Authorpreneur 101
How to Become a Successful Pet Author and Grow Your Business

THANK YOU FOR READING!

As the author of this book, I appreciate you buying and reading it. I hope you found the information useful and are on your way to becoming a successful pet author.

I would be grateful if you would leave a helpful book review, either with your favorite book distributor or with Amazon.

Thank you,

Wendy Van de Poll, MS, CEOL

Best-selling and Award-winning Author, Writing Coach, Animal Advocate

www.wendyvandepoll.com

For all of Wendy Van de Poll's books, please visit:
https:amazon.com/author/wendyvandepoll

Check out my Free Gift that Goes with This Book
https://wendyvandepoll.com/pet-authorpreneur-free-checklist

ALSO BY WENDY VAN DE POLL

The Pet Biz Series

Pet Blogging 101

Pet Jobs 101

Pet Authorpreneur 101

Pet Bereavement Series

My Dog Is Dying: What Do I Do?

My Dog Has Died: What Do I Do?

My Cat Is Dying: What Do I Do?

My Cat Has Died: What Do I Do?

Healing a Child's Pet Loss Grief

The Pet Professional's Guide to Pet Loss

Pet Loss Poems: To Heal Your Heart and Soul

Human-Animal Books

Animal Wisdom: Conversations From The Heart Between Animals and Their People

Free Book

Healing Your Heart From Pet Loss Grief

Children's Picture Books

The Adventures of Ms. Addie Pants Series
The Rescue
The Ice Storm
New Friends
Off to School

To receive notification when more books are published, please go to:

https://wendyvandepoll.com

We will add you to the mailing list after you download your free gift.

A Success Checklist to Become a Successful Pet Author and Grow Your Business

https://wendyvandepoll.com/pet-authorpreneur-free-checklist

You can also find my books on Amazon:

https://amazon.com/author/wendyvandepoll

www.ingramcontent.com/pod-product-compliance
Lightning Source LLC
Chambersburg PA
CBHW030000110526
44587CB00011BA/916